797,885 Books

are available to read at

Forgotten Books

www.ForgottenBooks.com

Forgotten Books' App
Available for mobile, tablet & eReader

ISBN 978-1-330-72031-8
PIBN 10096716

This book is a reproduction of an important historical work. Forgotten Books uses
state-of-the-art technology to digitally reconstruct the work, preserving the original format
whilst repairing imperfections present in the aged copy. In rare cases, an imperfection in
the original, such as a blemish or missing page, may be replicated in our edition. We do,
however, repair the vast majority of imperfections successfully; any imperfections that
remain are intentionally left to preserve the state of such historical works.

Forgotten Books is a registered trademark of FB &c Ltd.
Copyright © 2017 FB &c Ltd.
FB &c Ltd, Dalton House, 60 Windsor Avenue, London, SW19 2RR.
Company number 08720141. Registered in England and Wales.

For support please visit www.forgottenbooks.com

1 MONTH OF
FREE
READING

at

www.ForgottenBooks.com

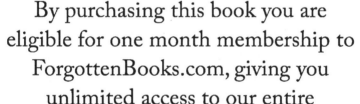

By purchasing this book you are eligible for one month membership to ForgottenBooks.com, giving you unlimited access to our entire collection of over 700,000 titles via our web site and mobile apps.

To claim your free month visit:
www.forgottenbooks.com/free96716

* Offer is valid for 45 days from date of purchase. Terms and conditions apply.

English
Français
Deutsche
Italiano
Español
Português

www.forgottenbooks.com

Mythology Photography **Fiction**
Fishing Christianity **Art** Cooking
Essays Buddhism Freemasonry
Medicine **Biology** Music **Ancient**
Egypt Evolution Carpentry Physics
Dance Geology **Mathematics** Fitness
Shakespeare **Folklore** Yoga Marketing
Confidence Immortality Biographies
Poetry **Psychology** Witchcraft
Electronics Chemistry History **Law**
Accounting **Philosophy** Anthropology
Alchemy Drama Quantum Mechanics
Atheism Sexual Health **Ancient History**
Entrepreneurship Languages Sport
Paleontology Needlework Islam
Metaphysics Investment Archaeology
Parenting Statistics Criminology
Motivational

CONTENTS

LIST OF ILLUSTRATIONS

List of Illustrations

NEW YEAR'S DAY

NEW YEAR'S DAY

"Full knee-deep lies the winter snow,
And the winter winds are wearily sighing:
Toll ye the church bells sad and slow,
And tread softly and speak low,
For the old year lies a-dying.

" . . . And let him in
That standeth there alone,
And waiteth at the door.
There's a new foot on the floor, my friend,
And a new face at the door, my friend,
A new face at the door."

— TENNYSON.

THE YEAR'S FESTIVALS

———◆———

NEW YEAR'S DAY

"The old year and the new year meet,
And one goes back to God again,
And one stays on for joy or pain."

NOTHING shows the character of a people more truly than the manner in which it observes its holidays, and the kind of amusements followed by a nation is a fairly true index to its degree of moral development.

The recreations of a rude and primitive nation must inevitably be limited to sensuous expressions, however they may be modified by climate and national customs; and in the earlier stages of civilization the main features of customs expressing the play instinct are strikingly similar the world over.

It is said that nothing is so difficult to control as popular customs which have reference to the enjoyments of a people, for that portion of its nature which craves pleasure is bound to be satisfied upon every possible occasion, and with every plausible excuse.

For many centuries the pagan games survived the gods in whose honor they were first instituted; and, more willing to surrender their worn-out religion than the amusements connected with it, Christianity could be made attractive to the ancient heathen only by allowing them to bring into their new faith many of their old pagan amusements and pastimes.

In very early times man discovered his instinct for sport, also that he was a gregarious animal, and that to enjoy himself fully, a man must meet with his fellows and share with them his recreations. As a result certain days were given up to this purpose.

Festival days have been established, some through natural causes, others arbitrarily, and still others by some event connected with the religious life of the people.

Our custom of celebrating New Year's Day is centuries old, and began with the ancient Germans, whose new year was established quite naturally, as a result of changing seasons.

The German year was at first divided loosely into winter and summer; reckoning the year by winters, and counting the winter with the following summer as one year. In Germany winter actually begins about the middle of November, when the ground begins to freeze, when snowfalls are frequent, and when it is no longer possible for cattle, horses, and sheep to be left on the pasture-lands to find their own food.

The early Germans, being cattle-keeping tribes, were compelled by this change to alter completely all their summer habits; and this marked, in a most definite way, the beginning of a new season. Around this time of harvest and flock-gathering grew up, naturally enough, certain festivities. among the people who had separated during the summer months, but who now collected in their rude winter shelters. This old Germanic division of the year, with its attendant festivities, is preserved in the legal institutions of the country, in popular tradition, in folk-lore, in the still existing rustic customs of festivals and bonfires, and in the religious habits. The amusements of this time were distinctly colored by the imaginative, simple German character, and so satisfied the universal need, that many of them, with modifications, were adopted by the other nations.

We have a glimpse of one of these old

German feasts, the first of which we have any trace. In the year 14, Germanicus was fighting some German tribes just to give his soldiers a little exercise before he withdrew into winter quarters; and being told by one of his scouts that a certain night was a festival-night for the Germans, when they would be absorbed in drinking and feasting, he rushed upon the village, and completely surprising it, captured all its inhabitants.

No mention is made of a New Year's observance again, until near the close of the sixth century, when St. Martin had become a great saint of the Church, and the date of his death, November 11th, had become the day for commemorating the beginning of the new year. Thus the festive season, which had heretofore been dependent upon a difference of temperature and other changes of nature, was attached to a fixed date. This was kept not only with the usual ceremonies, but with those which

grew out of ideas connected with St.
Martin, who soon became very popular; and
the celebration of Martinmas quickly spread
into Gaul and Britain.

While in Germany Martinmas and New
Year's Day were identical, the Romans were
reckoning the first of January as the beginning of the new year, according to the
Roman calendar, which is usually attributed
to Numa Pompilius. Numa, it is said, being
an impulsive despot, and having decreed
that the year should begin just then, when
the mood was upon him, added two new
months to the ten, into which the year had
been previously divided, and called the first
Januarius, in honor of Janus, the deity supposed to preside over open doors, and who
might naturally be interested in the opening
of the new year.

This god is represented by the Romans
as a man with two faces, one looking backward and the other forward, implying that

he stood between the past and the future year, regarding both.

An English poet has given us his picture of this old Roman god:

> "Hark, the cock crows, and yon bright star
> Tells us the day himself's not far;
> With him old Janus doth appear,
> Peeping into the future year
> With such a look as seems to say
> The prospect is not good that way.
> But stay! but stay! Methinks my sight
> Better informed by clearer light.
> His reversed face doth show distaste
> And frown upon the ills are past.
> But that which this way looks is clear,
> And smiles upon the new-born year."

With the invasion of the Romans came Roman customs, which were slowly adopted by the German people. Of course, Roman festive occasions were the first to be regarded, and gradually into the German feast-days crept a new element, none the less welcome because introduced by the conquering nation. These celebrations growing more and more popular each year, reached their height in the extravagant expressions of merriment and good cheer at Martinmas; but after the Julian calendar was generally accepted, it could not fail that usages having special reference to the beginning of the new year, in the observance of Martinmas, should be gradually transferred to the first of January. Comparatively modern New Year's customs have still retained something of the character of the old Martinmas festivities, which were often accompanied by very childish and grotesque performances.

Eating and drinking has ever been a favorite pastime, and much of this was done in honor of St. Martin. No wonder he is called the "drunken saint," nor do we marvel at the invention of a Martin goose. An old votive has said: "Firstly, they praise St. Martin with good wine and geese until they are drunk. Unblessed the house that has not a goose to eat that night; then they also tap their new wines which they have kept so far."

There was also a song dedicated to St. Martin for the benefit of the musical revellers, and St. Martin fires, — public bonfires around which the crowds gathered and when boys sang:

> "Stoocht vyer mackt vyer:
> Sinte Marten komt hier
> Met syne bloote armen;
> Hy sonde hem geerne warmen."[1]

This convenient saint was made useful by some who were more crafty than reverent. The story goes that a rich farmer and his people got drunk in honor of Saint Martin. A thief broke into the stable, and when sur-

---

[1] "Stoke the fire, make the fire:
Since St. Martin comes here
With his bare arms,
He would gladly warm them."

prised by the dazed farmer shook off his
clothes, assumed a humble attitude, and pre-
tended to be St. Martin. The credulous
farmer went on with his banquet, and in
the morning found his stable empty.

St. Martin's game gives us an idea of
the rough sport enjoyed by the crowds in
the public square, and is described thus:
" The people enclosed in a circuit two wild
boars, which tore each other to pieces. The
meat was divided among the people, the best
bits being given to the authorities." One
writer quaintly says: " We Germans think
St. Martin's the time when people should be
gay and banquet more than on other seasons
of the year; perhaps for the sake of the
new wine; then people roast fat geese, all
the world rejoicing." And with the same
idea a popular rhyme reads:

" Auff Martini schlacht man fliste Schwein
Und wird allda der Most zu Wein."

("On St. Martin's Day one slaughters busily, swine,
And then the must[1] is changed to wine.")

To add zest to the occasion, on St. Martin's Eve the devil was allowed free play, and many stories are told by the fearful, superstitious ones, of his walking about in the earth. On one Martinmas Eve, "in the shape of a man dressed in a long wolf-skin coat, he appeared before a young fellow, and raged about in such fashion, all the persons witnessing had to be brought to the high altar for protection." As children listen at the door and whisper "Wolves!" to induce delightful shivers of fear, so these people, not content with the plain pleasures of goose and wine, were exhausting the delights of fancy. Imaginations were doubtless unchecked as well as the evil one, and it was much more exciting to rush to high altars, screaming for protection, than to in-

[1] Unfermented wine — grape-juice.

vestigate this very commonplace devil. If a thief could successfully palm himself off as good St. Martin, surely even a harmless man might play at being a Martinmas devil.

This season marked a change in the domestic arrangements. House servants changed places at Martinmas, and farm hands began the new year under new masters; and there are still recollections of St. Martin's as being the old German New Year, for instead of saying, " A man has lived through many years," the people say, " The man has helped to eat many a St. Martin goose."

The old lines, " Iss Gäuss Martini, trink Wein ad circulum anni " (Eat goose-meat on St. Martin's Day, drink wine all the year round), refer to the beginning of the new year, when people drank good luck to a new twelvemonth.

While the celebration of Martinmas as the beginning of a new year was waning in

Germany and other countries, the first of January as New Year's Day was taking to itself much of the Martinmas spirit of jollity, and there were added to those customs already established variations which grew out of usages peculiar to different localities.

At New Year's Eve, superstitious people, girt with their swords, sat down on the roofs of their houses to discover what good and bad things would come with the New Year. Others knelt down at a cross-road on a cowhide to listen for oracles.

An early Roman custom was that of presenting branches of trees for the sake of good luck in the coming year. Our custom of decorating our houses and churches with laurel and evergreens is a remnant of this old Roman practice.

A good fifteenth-century churchman evidently regarded this custom doubtfully when he said: " Trimmyng of the Temples with hangynges, floures, boughs, and garlandes, was taken of the Heathene people whiche decked their Idoles and houses with suche arraye."

The custom of presenting and receiving gifts on St. Martin's Day became popular, as the ceremonies grew to be more elaborate; but later, when the rioting was carried to such an extent that it disturbed the public peace, and the police suppressed all expressions of hilarity, the gifts of Martinmas were gradually reduced to payments of rents to landlords, and tithes to the Church.

The New Year's gift no doubt originated with the Romans, for with them, giving and taking was carried to such an extravagant degree during all the three hundred and sixty-five days of the year, that Emperor Claudius prohibited the *demanding* of presents except on New Year's Day; but the practice continued for many years. In England and Scotland the sixteenth-century customs are numerous, and many of them are strangely childish.

In Scotland it was perfectly allowable to ask for a New Year's gift; and Henry III. of England is said to have extorted presents in plate and other valuables; while Queen Elizabeth's jewelry and wardrobe was almost wholly supplied from these gifts.

In the " Masque of Christmas," the character of " New Year's Gift " is described as appearing " in a blue coat, serving-man like, with an orange, and a sprig of rosemary on his head, his hat full of brooches, with a collar of gingerbread, his torch-bearer carrying a marchpane, with a bottle of wine on either arm." This motley fellow gives the complete early seventeenth-century thought of the New Year — the thoroughly material, eating and drinking, gift-taking, pleasure-loving New Year.

In old times gloves were popular, but in that age, very expensive New Year's presents, and when money was given instead of a gift, it was called " glove money."

Sir Thomas More, when Lord Chancellor, decided a case in favor of a certain lady, who, on the following New Year, presented him with a pair of gloves containing forty gold angels. Sir Thomas returned the coin with a note, saying: " Mistress, since it were against all good manners to refuse your New Year's gift, I am content to take your gloves, but as for the *lining,* I utterly refuse it."

The first metal pins were rough, hand-made affairs, but were considered rare pieces of workmanship compared with the skewers of bone and wood formerly used, and this invention was so important that during the reign of Henry VIII. a statute was passed called " An acte for the true making of Pynnes."

These new articles for the toilet made very agreeable gifts for ladies, and the money spent for these luxuries was called "pin money," a familiar expression to us, but used now with quite a different meaning.

The usual gift of country tenants to their landlords was a capon, as no common fowl was in keeping with this extraordinary feasting-time. This peasant gift is mentioned in the old rhyme:

> "When with low legs, and in a humble guise
> Ye offered up a capon-sacrifice
> Unto his Worship at the New Year's tide."

"His Worship" accepted this sacrifice as a part of his New Year, never thinking that his servant with "low legs and humble guise" might never have tasted good fat capon. The sympathies of Bishop Hall are clearly in favor of the swain who is forced to be generous, when in his satires he says:

> "Yet must he haunt his greedy landlord's hall
> With often presents at ech festivall;

With crammèd capons every New Year's morne,
Or with green cheeses when his sheep are shorne,
Or many maunds full of his mellow fruite."

Within his hall the landlord of old England made merry with his family, in feasting and drinking the famous wassail, which had become an important part of New Year's merrymaking. The head of the house called the members of his family around the bowl of spiced ale, and drank their healths, then passed it to the rest, who drank with the words " Wass hael " (" To your health ").

There is little doubt that the term wassail is found in the story of Vortigern and Rowena, the daughter of the old Jute chief Hengist. It is said that on Vortigern's first interview with the lady, she knelt before him, and, presenting a cup of wine, said, " Lord King, wacht heil! " (" Health to you "). As the Briton did not understand the language, he inquired the meaning of the words. He was told that they wished his

health, and that he should answer by saying *drinc heil.* He asked one of his men to
explain the custom, which he did. The
incident is described in the old English lines
of Robert de Brunne:

> "This is ther custom and her gest
> When thei are at the ale or fest.
> Ilk man that lovis quare him think
> Sall say *Wasseille,* and to him drink.
> He that bidis sallé say *Wassaile,*
> The other sall say again *Drinkhaille*
> That says *Wosseille* drinkis of the cop
> Kissand his fellaw he gives it up.
> The king said as the knight gan ken
> *Drinkheille,* smiland on Rouewén,
> Rouwen drank as hire list
> And gave the king, sine him kist.
> There was the first wassaille in dede,
> And that first of fame yede.
> Of that wassaille men told grete tale,
> And wassaile whan thei were at ale
> And drink heille to tham that drank;
> Thus was wassaile taen to thank."

The wassail of later times was not a
simple ale or wine, but was a mixed drink,

made with studied care as to ingredients and
flavor; the recipe for making it exceeds anything in our modern cook-books as an
example of intricate compounding. It contained eight kinds of spices, six bottles of
ale, sherry, or Madeira, twelve eggs, "well
whisked up," and various fruits. After
many processes of slow and brisk stirring,
simmering, skimming, gradual adding of ingredients, and pouring from one dish to
another, the mixture was boiled "till a fine
froth was obtained." Then, with the tossing
in of "twelve fine soft roasted apples," it was
sent up hot.

A favorite New Year's gift was an orange
stuck with cloves, which was used to float
in the wassail-bowl to add new and delicious
flavors.

The poorer classes were accustomed to call
upon their more favored neighbors after the
family health-drinking, with a bowl decked
with ribbons, to ask for contributions of

spiced ale, that they, as well as their landlords, might drink wassail. The old song
used by the Gloucestershire rustics, in their
rounds for ale, served to give voice to their
spirit of jollity, and to turn embarrassing
begging into an occasion to compliment the
host, the members of his family, and his
horses and cows. The doggerel runs:

"Wassail! Wassail! over the town,
Our toast it is white, our ale it is brown:
Our bowl it is made of the maplin-tree,
We be good fellows all; I drink to thee.

"Here's to Roan Dobbin, and to his right ear,
God send our maister a happy new year;
A happy new year as e'er I did see —
With my wassailing bowl I drink to thee.

"Here's to old Ewe-neck, and to his right eye,
God send our mistress a good Christmas pie:
A good Christmas pie as e'er I did see —
With my wassailing bowl I drink to thee.

"Here's to Filpail, and to her long tail,
God send our maister us never may fail
Of cup of good beer; I pray you draw near,
And then you shall hear our jolly wassail.

"Be here any maids, I suppose there be some;
Sure they will not let young men stand on the cold
    stone;
Sing hey O maids, come troll back the pin,
And the fairest maid in the house, let us all in.

"Come, butler, come bring us a bowl of the best:
I hope your soul in heaven may rest:
But if you do bring us a bowl of the small,
Then down fall butler, bowl, and all."

The spirit of good wishing was so broad
that it included not only the domestic animals, but even the fruit-trees; and there
existed the custom of " apple howling," when
troops of boys gathered in the orchards, and,
surrounding the apple-trees, sang:

"Stand fast root, bear well top,
    Pray God send us a good howling **crop;**
        Every twig, apples big;
        Every bough, apples enow;
        Hats full, caps full,
        Full quarter sacks full."

Then followed a chorus with an **accom**-
paniment of blaring cow-horns and the beat-
ing of tree-trunks.

An old English writer looked upon all the benefactions, health-drinkings, and other ceremonies, with evident suspicion, for he says:

"The 1st of January being raw, colde, and comfortlesse to such as have lost their money at dice at one of the Temples over-night, strange apparitions are like to be seen." And with reference to New Year's gifts, writes: " This day shall be given many more gifts than shall be asked for, and apples, egges, and oranges shall be lifted to a lofty rate; when a pome-water bestucke with a few rotten cloves shall be more worth than the honesty of a hypocrite; and halfe a dozen eggs of more estimation than the vowes of a strumpet.

" Poets shall this day get mightily by their pamphlets; for an hundred of elaborate lines shall be less esteemed in London than an hundred of Walfleet oysters at Cambridge."

The hospitality of New Year's tide is perversely interpreted by Seldon in his "Table Talks," who ungraciously says of the offering of wassail by women:

"At New Year's tide these wenches present you with a cup, and you must drink of a slabby stuff, but the meaning is, you must give them money ten times more than it is worth."

The custom of wassail drinking prevailed in the monasteries, as well as in private houses. Before the abbot at the head of the table was placed the huge bowl; the superior then drank to all, and each monk to the others, and so on down the table, each standing while drinking the health of his next neighbor. This ceremony is the origin of the loving-cup.

The Scots have a legend of the healing properties of wassail. "There was a collier, one William Hunter, who was cured in the year 1758 of an inveterate gout, by drinking freely of new ale, full of barm or yest. The poor man had been confined to his bed for a year and a half, having almost lost the use of his limbs. On New Year's Eve some of his friends came to make merry with him. Though he could not rise, he always took his share of ale as it passed round the company, and, in the end, became very drunk. The consequence was, that he had the use of his legs the next morning, and was able to walk about. He lived more than twenty years after this, and never had the slightest return of the malady."

The custom of drinking in the New Year with spiced drinks prevailed vigorously in Scotland until a very few years ago. Then, just before twelve o'clock, a " hot pint " was prepared, and at the stroke of midnight each member of the family drank " a good health and a happy New Year and many of them " to all the rest; then would follow handshaking and more good wishing and a dance

around the table, with a shouting of the song
to the tune of " Hey tuttie taitie " :

> " Weel may we a' be,
> Ill may we never see,
> Here's to the king
> And the gude companie! "

After this home drinking, the older members
of the household often took the hot kettle
to a neighbor's house, but if on the way they
were met by others bent on the same errand,
boisterous good wishes were again expressed,
and the " hot pint " went the rounds.

If you were the first one to enter your
neighbor's house after midnight, you brought
good luck to the family for the year, and
you were called the *first foot;* but to insure
the heartiest welcome, in addition to your
hot pint, you must come loaded with bread
and cheese and cakes, of which civility de-
manded that each member of the family
should partake. This custom is thoroughly
consistent with Scotch philosophy, which

shouting of the song

New Year's

FIRST-FOOTERS OF THE
OLDEN TIME

taught that you must share your neighbor's goods while you may, and is embodied in the old verse:

"Get up gude wife and binno sweir, (lazy)
And deal your cakes and cheese while you are here;
For the time will come when ye'll be dead
And neither need your cheese nor bread."

The custom of first-footing was so popular in Edinburgh, that at the hours about midnight the streets were thronged with rollicking, jovial people, and much good feeling existed among all classes.

Unfortunately this pleasant part of New Year's celebration was abolished through an event both surprising and disastrous. Some reckless young fellows decided that this was an occasion to despoil the unsuspecting first-footers of their watches and other valuables. The streets at that time being dark, or, at best, poorly lighted by lanterns, the young men agreed to "look out for white neck-cloths," thinking that the best way by which they could distinguish a gentleman who was likely to carry valuables. A great number had watches, money, and jewels taken, and the slightest resistance was encountered with such brutality that many died from the injuries received. This so outraged the community that as a punishment three of the young thieves were executed on the scene of riot; and the feeling was so wide-spread and lasting, that from that time first-footing with the hot pint ceased to be in vogue. .

There was, however, a first-footing independent of the wassail-bowl, and which was in no way affected by the riots of young thieves.

The young man who could meet a fresh, charming first-footer at the door was not only given the privilege of kissing her, but the good luck she brought him would win him a bride before another year came round. Though the position of doorkeeper was

much sought after by the laddies, it was not
without its drawbacks, for more than likely,
instead of meeting his blushing Peggy,
he was obliged to lead in his withered grand-
mother or a maiden aunt, the butt of a taunt-
ing, unmerciful company.

There are various old sayings connected
with New Year's Day. In an old English
tract we find this advice for January first:

"This month drink you no wine commixed with
    dregs;
Eat capons, and fat hens with dumpling legs."

Then it is bad luck to carry anything out
of the house before bringing something in,
according to this rhyme:

"Take out, then take in,
    Bad luck will begin;
    Take in, then take out,
    Good luck comes about."

The saying is still heard:

"In the North of England, at New Year's tide,
The days lengthen a cock's stride."

And:

> "If the grass grows in Janiveer,
>   It grows the worse for't all the year."

Another old saw is:

> "The blackest month of all the year,
>   Is the month of Janiveer."

In a few rural places the ringing in of New Year from the church belfries is now the only open demonstration of cheer at this anniversary, and nearly all of the old-time observances have fallen into disuse.

The custom once so general among gentlemen, of making rounds of calls upon New Year's Day, is now discontinued. This custom came down to us from the New Amsterdam Dutch, whose hospitality was limitless on New Year's Day; and the people of New York continued this social custom for several centuries.

The watch-meetings and midnight services in churches, and the gathering of young people, who get together to watch the old year out and the new year in, will probably be continued; for there is still that in us which impels us to sit up till after twelve o'clock on that mystic night, lest something supernatural takes place that we would miss by going to bed early. There is a remnant of the old superstition left in the modern civilized heart, which flavors of that which prompted the forefathers to climb on the roof to see what would happen on New Year's night.

With the inevitable growth into things spiritual we are no longer satisfied to remember this anniversary with a great deal to eat, very much more to drink, and with gifts extorted from our friends.

We generally talk about "New Year's resolutions," if we do not put them into practice, and some make the effort to shake themselves free from their old year's garment, worn and tattered and patched, in exchange for one which they hope to wear unspotted for a twelvemonth.

Of New Year's Day Charles Lamb said that no one, of whatever rank, can regard it with indifference. " Of all sounds of all bells," he says, " most solemn and touching is the peal which rings out the old year. I never hear it without a gathering up of my mind to a concentration of all the images that have diffused over the past twelve-month; all I have done or suffered, performed or neglected, in that regretted time. I begin to know its worth when a friend dies. It takes a personal color; nor was it a poetical flight in a contemporary when he exclaimed:

" 'I saw the skirts of the departing year.' "

The thoughts surrounding the old and new year have inspired poets to produce gems in verse. What can be more vivid than

the picture which Tennyson gives us in " The
Death of the Old Year "?

These words by Edith Thomas from the
mouth of Janus in a " New Year's Masque,"
suggest varied thought, and are full of
beautiful imagery :

"'Tis mine to guard the portal of the year,
To close or open to the seasons four
And to the importuning throng of days.
Sometimes I hear the tread of stormy feet,
Hoarse trumpet blasts, and loud assaulting blows,
And threats to pull my ancient fortress down;
But other times they come with flatteries smooth,
Entreating, 'Janus, Janus, let us in!'
I watchful stand; I will not turn the key
Until my glass and fingered dial stern
Declare the moment ripe. Two ways I look,
Two faces I present; one seamed with eld,
And gray with looking on the frozen past;
One fresh as morn, and fronting days to be.

．　．　．　．　．　．　．　．　．　．

Now while the surging, deep-toned bells lament
The passèd year, e'er fickle, they shall change
Their solemn burden for a round of joy,
Chiming the praises of the year new-crowned."

TWELFTH NIGHT

TWELFTH NIGHT

"THE THREE KINGS

"Three Kings came riding from far away,
  Melchior, and Gaspar, and Baltasar;
Three Wise Men out of the East were they,
And they travelled by night and they slept by day,
  For their guide was a beautiful, wonderful star.

.   .   .   .

"And the Three Kings rode through the gate and
    the guard,
  Through the street till their horses turned
And neighed as they entered the great inn-yard;
But the windows were closed and the doors were
    barred,
  And only a light in the stable burned.

"And cradled there in the scented hay,
  In the air made sweet by the breath of kine,
The little child in the manger lay,
The child that would be king one day
  Of a kingdom not human but divine."

— LONGFELLOW.

TWELFTH NIGHT

" At his birth a star
Unseen before in Heaven proclaims Him come;
And guides the Eastern sages, who inquire
His place, to offer incense, myrrh, and gold."
— MILTON.

" A jolly
Verse crowned with ivy and with holly;
That tells of winter's tales and mirth
That milk-maids make about the hearth;
Of Twelfth-tide cakes, of peas and beans,
Wherewith ye make those merry scenes,
Whenas ye choose your king and queen,
And cry out, " Hey for our town green!"
— HERRICK.

THE climax of that festival season inaugurated on Christmas Eve is reached on Twelfth Day, the sixth of January, which is also the Church feast of the Epiphany.

The chief event commemorated is the visit of the three Magi, or Wise Men of

39

the East, to the infant Saviour.   There are
other references, as the baptism of our Lord,
and his miraculous power displayed at the
marriage at Cana of Galilee, and the feed-
ing of the five thousand, which are said to
have occurred on this date.   But these points
are of minor importance on this day of the
" Feast of Three Kings," as it is called in
the Latin Church, for, originally, all the
ceremonies had particular reference to the
visit of the " Three Kings," as they came
to be called.

The story had been elaborated in its de-
tails by the help of tradition and imagination, and these men were considered to have
been royal personages, named Melchior, Caspar, and Balthasar, 'descended respectively
from Shem, Ham, and Japheth, and were
the first of the heathen world to do homage
to Christ.   They were guided by the blazing
star in the East, and reached " the place
where the young child lay " just twelve days

after his birth. Melchior brought gold in testimony of Christ's royalty, Caspar brought frankincense in token of his divinity, and Balthasar brought myrrh in allusion to the sorrows which the Divine One had taken upon himself by becoming man.

These remarkable strangers have been highly honored, and their deed of devotion being the occasion of one of the most firmly established festival days of the Church, they are not likely ever to be forgotten. Whence they came and whither they went remains a mystery, but their pilgrimage to the cradle of the Christ-Child was enough to warm the heart of the world to them for all the ages following.

The day is sometimes called the "Feast of the Star," and has been celebrated under that name in the Church, and as a sacred festival in other places.

The name Twelfth Night is a relic of the time when the period of twenty-four hours

was reckoned from sunset to sunset, and
night meant not only a night but the day
following.

A little dramatic service called the " Feast
of the Star " was acted in the churches, in
the Middle Ages. " Three priests, clothed as
kings, with their servants carrying offerings, met from different directions before
the altar. The middle one, who came from
the east, pointed with his staff to a star.
A dialogue then ensued; and after kissing
each other, they began to sing, ' Let us go
and inquire;' after which, the precentor
began a responsory, ' Let the Magi come.'
A procession then commenced, and as soon
as it began to enter the nave, a crown, with
a star, resembling a cross, was lighted up
and pointed out to the Magi with the words,
' Behold the Star in the East.' This being
concluded, two priests, standing at each
side of the altar, answered meekly, ' We
are those whom you seek;' and, drawing a

curtain, shewed them a child, whom, falling down, they worshipped. Then the servants made the offerings of gold, frankincense, and myrrh, which were divided among the priests. The Magi, meanwhile, continued praying till they dropped asleep; then a boy, clothed in an alb, like an angel, addressed them with ' All things which the prophets said are fulfilled.' The festival concluded with a chanting service." This description shows us how slightly the celebration of Twelfth Night, in mediæval times, departed from the purely religious thought. Later it became much more secular.

At Milan, in 1336, the *Festival of the Three Kings* was celebrated in a spectacular manner, paying attention to the externals of Christianity, as was the tendency of the Middle Ages; reminding one of the whited sepulchre of Scripture reference. " The three kings appeared, crowned, on three great horses richly habited, surrounded by

pages, body-guards, and an innumerable
retinue. A golden star was exhibited in the
sky going before them. They proceeded to
the pillars of St. Lawrence, where King
Herod was represented, with his scribes and
wise men.

" The three kings ask Herod where Christ
should be born, and his wise men, having
consulted their books, answer, at Bethle-
hem. On which the three kings, with their
golden crowns, having in their hands golden
cups filled with frankincense, myrrh, and
gold, the star going before, marched to the
Church of St. Eustorgius, with all their attendants, preceded by trumpets, horns, asses,
baboons, and a great variety of animals.
In the church, on one side of the high altar,
there was a manger with an ox and ass,
and in it the infant Christ in the arms of his
mother. Here the three kings offer him
gifts. The concourse of people, of knights,

ladies, and ecclesiastics, was such as was never before beheld."

This rather involved description gives us a picture of a very motley crowd. One can well believe that the scene was impressive, though the quantity of live stock suggests to the light mind of the present day some recollections of a circus parade. A baboon never laughs, to be sure, but he seems a bit out of place in a religious procession.

Robert Herrick, who wrote during the first half of the seventeenth century, has left us a sweet, quaint little poem, which combines the devotion to the Christ-Child with a suggestion of the festive customs of the time:

"THE STAR SONG: A CAROLL TO THE KING

"SUNG AT WHITE-HALL.

"*The flourish of musick — then followed the Song.*
Tell us, thou clere and heavenly Tongue,
Where is the Babe but lately sprung?
Lies he the lillie-banks among?

"Or say if this new Birth of ours
Sleeps, laid within some ark of flowers,
Spangled with deaw-lights? Thou canst cleere
All doubts, and manifest the where.

"Declare to us, bright star, if we shall seek
Him in the morning's blushing cheek,
Or search the beds of spices through,
To find him out?

" STÀR.

"No, this ye need not do:
  But onely come, and see Him rest
  A princely Babe in's mother's brest.

" CHORUS.

"He's seen! He's seen! Why then a round
Let's kisse the sweet and holy ground,
And all rejoyce that we have found
A King, before conception crown'd.

"Come then, come then, and let us bring
Unto our prettie Twelfth-Tide King
Each one his severall offering.

"And when night comes, wee'l give him wassailing;
And that his treble honors may be seen,
Wee'l chuse him King and make his mother queen."

There were influences of a more festive
and frivolous nature abroad in the land
than the story of the three Magi, and the
customs of Twelfth Night were, many of
them, far from dignified or solemn. Some
have tried to identify the date with that of
the old Saturnalia, but it seems a useless
task to attempt anything of the kind, when
the days, months, and years were not the
same in all parts of the civilized world, and
it is not likely that the identity of dates
could be proved. Of course, the old social
customs had their effect upon the surrounding nations, as surely as to-day our liter-
ature and art are influenced by Greece and
Rome, now so long dead.

The character of the Twelfth-Night celebration lost, in time, much of its religious
tone, and took a more easy, festive air,
though the Magi were always remembered,
in form, at least. The kings of England,
down to the time of the Georges, went with

their courtiers to church, on Twelfth Day, with offerings of gold, frankincense, and myrrh.

As a popular feast-day, Twelfth Day stands second only to Christmas. Being at the end of that holiday-time, the "twelve days of Christmas," it would seem that the people let their spirits loose for a final revel, as if there would never be another play-day as far in the future as they could see. Even then, some seemed unable to terminate their sports, and went on feasting till Candlemas Day — the second of February; but that was practised, they say, "only among the vulgar." The athletes of our own day would find it wearisome to carouse for nearly two weeks, while ordinary mortals would lie by the wayside in heaps of wreckage, if they attempted one of those sixteenth century Christmas festivals, twenty days in extent.

The one thing peculiar to Twelfth-Night revels in all lands, was the choosing of a

Twelfth Night

THE BEAN-CAKE KING

king of the feast by means of a bean hidden in a cake. This "bean-cake king" is the most distinctive feature of the occasion. Around him the other persons and performances revolve as satellites of lesser glory. In many a history, diary, poem, and story do we find reference to this old custom. It was a common gambol at the commencement of the eighteenth century, at the English universities and elsewhere, to give the name of king or queen to that person whose luck it was to choose the piece of a divided cake, which was honored above all the others by having a bean in it.

Sometimes a coin was used instead of a bean. A detailed account of election and the subsequent ceremonies, as they occurred before the year 1620, is taken from an old authority as follows:

" Here we have the materials of the cake, which are flour, honey, ginger, and pepper. One is made for each family. The maker thrusts in, at random, a small coin as she is kneading it. When it is baked, it is divided into as many parts as there are persons in the family. It is distributed, and each has his share. Portions of it are also assigned to Christ, the Virgin, and the three Magi, which are given away in alms. Whoever finds the piece of coin in his share, is saluted by all as king, and, being placed on a seat or throne, is thrice lifted aloft with joyful acclamations. He holds a piece of chalk in his right hand, and each time he is lifted up, makes a cross on the ceiling. These crosses are thought to prevent many evils, and are much revered."

A queen was chosen by the king, or, in some cases, by a " peaze " found in the cake. The host and hostess were often, more by design than accident, appointed king and queen. These choose other members of the company to be ministers of state, maids of honor, or ladies of the bedchamber. According to Twelfth-Day law, each supported his character till midnight. The king appointed one of the company as fool for the evening, and it was his pleasant mission to " keep the table in a roar." This could not have been difficult under the circumstances.

The chief entertainment and delight of the evening was, of course, drinking. The king was the first to raise his glass, and at that moment the company shouted, " The king drinks! " and impetuously followed his lead. The healths of all must be drunk, and by the time midnight arrived, especially at the end of a twelve days'· revel, they must have been a very sodden company indeed.

In France it seems to have been the custom for the " bean-cake king " to pay the cost of his banquet. This is referred to incidentally in an English political tract published in 1651 : " Verily, I think they make use of kings as the French on Epiphany Day use their Roy de la Fehve, or King of the

Bean; whom, after they have honored with
drinking of his health, and shouting aloud,
'Le Roy boit! Le Roy boit!' they make pay
for all the reckoning, not leaving him sometimes one penny, rather than that the exhor-
bitance of their debosh should not be satisfied
to the full."

The following description of a Twelfth-
Day revel shows how it was conducted in
the halls of the country gentry and substantial yeomanry in England in the reigns
of Elizabeth and James I.

The breakfast on Twelfth Day is directed
to be of brawn, mustard, and malmsey; the
dinner of two courses, to be served in the
hall, and after the first course " cometh in the
Master of the Game, apparelled in green
velvet, and the Ranger of the Forest, also
in a green suit of satten; bearing in his hand
a green bow and divers arrows, with either
of them a hunting-horn about their necks:
blowing together three blasts of venery, they

Twelfth Night

REVELS IN AN OLD ENGLISH
COUNTRY HOUSE

pace round about the fire three times. Then
the Master of the Game maketh three cour-
tesies, kneels down, and petitions to be admitted into the service of the Lord of the
Feast.

" This ceremony performed, a huntsman
cometh into the hall, with a fox and a purse-
net, with a cat, both bound at the end of
a staff; and with them nine or ten couple
of hounds, with the blowing of hunting-
horns. And the fox and the cat are by the
hounds set upon and killed beneath the fire."
.(Poor pussy — you were not fair game!)
" This sport finished, the Marshal placeth
them in their several appointed places."

After the second course " the antientest
of the Masters of the Revels singeth a song
with the assistance of others there present; "
and after some repose and revels, supper is
served in the hall, and being ended, " the
Marshall presenteth himself with drums
afore him, mounted upon a scaffold, borne

by four men; and goeth three times round
the harthe, crying out aloud, ' A Lord, a
Lord!' then he descendeth and goeth to
dance. This done, the Lord of Misrule ad-
dresseth himself to the Banquet; which
ended with some minstralsye, mirth, and
dancing, every man departeth to rest."

Viewed in the cold light of reason, it
would appear that it was time for " every
man to depart to rest," as about the only
thing left for him to do.

In " Hesperides," published by Robert
Herrick in 1648, there is a curious and pleasing account of the Twelfth-Night proceedings as we may suppose them to have
occurred in private families:

"TWELFTH NIGHT; OR, KING AND QUEEN

> " Now, the mirth comes
> 　With the cake full of plums,
> Where Beane's the king of the sport here;
> 　·Beside, we must know,
> 　The Pea also
> Must revell, as Queene, in the court here.

"Begin then to chuse
This night as ye use,
Who shall for the present delight here,
Be a King by the lot,
And who shall not
Be Twelfe-day Queene for the night here.

"Which knowne, let us make
Joy-sops with the cake;
And let not a man then be seen here,
Who unurged will not drinke
To the base from the brink
A health to the King and the Queene here.

"Next crowne the bowle full
With gentle lambs-wooll;
Adde sugar, nutmeg and ginger,
With store of ale too;
And thus ye must doe
To make the *Wassaile* a swinger.

"Give then to the King
And Queene wassailing;
And though with ale ye be whet here:
Yet part ye from hence
As free from offence
As when ye innocent met here."

In Miss Strickland's "Queens of Scotland" is a pretty account of the celebration

of Twelfth Night, 1563, by Mary, Queen
of Scots, at Holyrood. They cast lots, and
Mary Flemming, one of the "Queen's
Maries," was "Queen of the Bean," and her
royal mistress dressed her in her own gorgeous robes, and, by the report of a wit-
ness, she was a beautiful sight indeed. He
says: "Two such sights, in one state, in
so good accord, I believe was never seen,
as to behold two worthy queens, possessing
without envy, one kingdom, both upon one
day. My pen staggereth, my hand faileth,
further to write. . . ."

Some of the ceremonies of Twelfth Day
resembled those of Christmas and New
Year's. Being a continuation of the same
celebration, it is not strange that there should
have been no distinct line drawn to confine
the practices which might have been common to many feasts. For instance, "wassailing the trees" was a ceremony which might
have been seen on any one of these three

chief days of the Christmas festival, but was, at times and places, certainly confined to Twelfth Night.

Thus we find in the glossary to the Exmoor dialect, " Watsail, a drinking-song, sung on Twelfth-Day Eve, throwing toast to the apple-trees, in order to have a fruitful year; which seems to be a relic of the heathen sacrifice to Pomona."

The same was done in Herefordshire under the name of Wassailing. At the approach of evening on the vigil of Twelfth Day, the farmers, with their friends and servants, meet together, and about six o'clock walk out to a field where wheat is growing. In the highest part of the ground, twelve small fires and one large one are lighted. The attendants, headed by the master of the family, pledge the company in old cider, which circulates freely on these occasions. A circle is formed around the large fire, when a general shout and hallooing takes place, which you hear answered from all the adjacent villages and fields. Sometimes fifty or sixty of these fires may be seen at a time. After the fires begin to die, the company return home, where the housewife and her maids are preparing a good supper. A large cake is always provided with a hole in the centre. After supper they all go to the wain-house, where they fill a cup with strong ale, and the bailiff stands opposite the first of the oxen, and pledges him in a toast; the company follow his example. The cake is then slipped on the horn of the ox, and then some one tickles him to make him toss his head. If he throws the cake behind him, it becomes the perquisite of the mistress; if he throws it before him, it is the bailiff who claims it.

The people then return to the house and find it locked, nor will it open to them till some joyous songs are sung. On being admitted, a scene of mirth and jollity follows, which lasts the greater part of the night.

Another description says: "After they have drank a chearful glass to their master's health, and success to the future harvest, they return home and feast on cakes made of caraways, soaked in cyder, which they claim as a reward for their past labor in sowing the grain. This seems to resemble a custom of the ancient Danes, who, in their addresses to their rural deities, emptied, on every invocation, a cup in honor of them."

In Yorkshire it was customary for many families, on the *Twelfth Eve of Christmas,* to invite their relations, friends, and neighbors to their houses to play at cards, and to partake of a supper of which mince pies were indispensable; and after supper the wassail-bowl was brought in, and every one partook, by skimming out and eating a roasted apple, then drinking the healths of the company from the bowl.

The ingredients of the wassail, — ale, sugar, nutmeg, roasted apples, and a variety of other things, was usually called *Lamb's Wool*, and the night on which it was drank was commonly called *Wassail Eve*.

We have an ingenuous description of Twelfth Night written in 1623: " This day, about the hours from five to ten, yea, in some places till midnight well nigh, will be such a massacre of spice-bread, that ere the next day at noone, a two-penny browne loafe will set twenty poore folkes' teeth on edge, which hungry humor will hold so violent, that a number of good fellowes will not refuse to give a statute marchant of all the lands and goods they enjoy, for half-a-crowne's worth of two-penny pasties. On this night much masking in the Strand, Cheapside, Holburne, or Fleet-Street."

A side-light on the festive nature of Twelfth Night is cast by the revelations of St. Distaff's Day, which is the day following, and Plough Monday. Again, Herrick has given us a glimpse of the life of his time in a short poem called " St. Distaff's Day; or, The Morrow after Twelfth Day." It begins :

> " Partly work and partly play
> Ye must on St. Distaff's Day."

And ends :

> " And next morrow, every one
> To his owne vocation."

The idea seems to be to sober off gradually, as is further shown by these lines referring to Plough Monday, which was the Monday following Twelfth Day :

> " Good huswives, whom God hath enriched ynough,
> forget not the feasts that belong to the plough.
> The meaning is only to joy and be glad,
> for comfort with labor, is fit to be had."

Then is added :

> " Plough-Munday, next after that Twelfth-Tide is
>   past
> bids out, with the plough, the worst husband is last :

If ploughman get hatchet or whip to the skreene,
  maids loveth their cocke, if no water be seene."

These lines allude to a custom prevalent in the sixteenth and seventeenth centuries, which is explained thus:

" After Christmas (which formerly, during the twelve days, was a time of very little work), every gentleman feasted the farmers, and every farmer their servants and task-men. Plough Monday puts them in mind of their business.

" In the morning the men and maid servants strive who shall shew their diligence in rising earliest; if the ploughman can get his whip, his plough-staff, hatchet, or anything that he wants in the field, by the fireside, before the maide hath got her kettle on, then the maide looseth her Shrovetide cock, and it wholly belongs to the men. Thus did our forefathers strive to allure youth to their duty, and provided innocent mirth, as well as labor. On this Plough

Monday they have a good supper and some strong drink, that they might not go immediately out of one extreme into another."

The celebration of Twelfth Night with the elegant and costly Twelfth-cake has much declined in the last half-century. In former days the confectioners' shops were filled with cakes of all sizes for this special purpose. One of the oldest shops in London is pointed out as being established in the time of George I., by Mr. Lucas Birch, who was succeeded by his son. The sign, " Birch, Birch & Co.," is still over the door. The younger Birch was once lord mayor. He still retained his shop, however, and annually sent a present of a Twelfth-cake to the Mansion House, which is just opposite.

The custom of masking has come down to the present day, and in some places in England we hear of an occasional Twelfth-cake, and King of the Bean, and of Twelfth-Night balls or masques held here and there.

But the custom is not of any material importance in our country. It simply gives an excuse for a little variety in the gaiety of the winter season, and an occasion to call a good time by some new name.

The youngsters who dance at a Twelfth-Night party do not know a wheat-field from a corn-bin, and as for " wassailing " an apple-tree, a weeping-willow would be likely to mislead them. But they can crown one of their number king, and deck themselves with long ears, or horns, or a butterfly's wings, and have as jolly a time as did their ancestors in England or France or Germany, two or three hundred years ago.

ST. VALENTINE'S DAY

ST. VALENTINE'S DAY

"Nature, the Vicar of the Almighty Lord
That hot, cold, hevie, light, moist and drie
Hath knit, by even number of accord,
In casie voice, began to speak and say,
Foules, take hede of my sentence I pray,
And for your own ease, in fordring of your nede,
As fast as I may speak, I will me spede.
Ye know well, how on St. Valentine's Day,
By my statute, and through my governance
Ye doe chese your mates, and after fly away
With hem, as I pricke you with pleasaunce."

— CHAUCER.

St. Valentine's Day

THE VALENTINE

ST. VALENTINE'S DAY

" Oft have I heard both youths and virgins say
 Birds chuse their mates, and couple too, this day:
 But by their flight I never can divine,
 When I shall couple with my valentine."
        — HERRICK.

  "To-morrow is St. Valentine's Day,
   All in the morning betime,
   And I a maid at your window
   To be your Valentine."

THUS sings Polonius' mad daughter as
the ghost of former St. Valentine Days
flits through the vacant chambers of her
mind. She has caught just an instant's
consciousness of what her words really
mean; then it escapes her, leaving only an
impression that, somehow, to-day is the day
set apart for all true lovers, when they may

devote themselves to each other by right, in the name of the good saint.

With us the day of St. Valentine means hardly more than it did to Ophelia, but there is still left an influence which has been given to it, by the many generations of young lovers, who have made the day their own, and who have surrounded it with an atmosphere distinctly amorous. In these days we get but a breath of this; just a suggestion of lavender or a wave of musk that still hovers around the old, yellow, crumpled love-missives that have survived the years, and that our great-grandmothers received and blushingly opened, and read with palpitating hearts.

It seems strange that this plain little valentine of two hundred years ago should have caused a tremor; the paper is coarse and brownish, not an attempt at ornamentation, with just a few lines of crude verse written in a stiff, conventional hand. But after all, it was written from the full heart of some seventeenth century grandfather with much feeling and in dead earnest.

Another valentine shows just a little more freedom, and gives evidence of a more recent date. This is a circle of paper which has been folded and cut into fanciful designs.

There is an angular, lacy edge, and four hearts cut with points toward the centre, and radiating between the hearts are some very prettily written things, four flattering sentiments that would please even the demurest maiden.

Then there are others more courageously done. There are hearts drawn, modest little ones, to be sure, and very unsymmetrical, but unmistakably hearts, with a few deformed doves flying about, some carrying in their bills scrolls and ribbons with little sentiments written upon them, while others sit upon nothing, and suggest — at least, the artist intended to suggest — billing and cooing.

With specimens of the valentines which have been circulated for hundreds of years, one needs no calendar to tell the relative date. With time grew boldness of thought and elaborateness of execution. After the heart and dove valentines came those decorated with larger hearts outlined in red ink, and not only outlined but done in solid, gory colors all bestuck with arrows. The verses attached also grew in fervor, and when an ardent lover failed to find expression for his feelings in proper original verse, he had recourse to " The Young Man's Valentine Writer," a book of verses suited to all sorts and conditions of men and women, where one could find any or all of his sentiments elaborately expressed. The first book of this kind was printed in 1797, but before that time a young fellow was sometimes hard put to write his ideas to suit himself and his lady fair. The lover of 1775 was more concerned with the thought than with the subtilty of expression, when his pent-up feelings burst forth with, "O my love, my dear love pretty! How I love you!" illustrated with a great red heart spitted upon an arrow.

For him who preferred to write in verse it was a fortunate thing that *heart* and *dart* rhymed so perfectly. They were just the words he needed, and were always useful, no matter how much other material he had at hand.

"A loving heart" always went well with "A poisoned dart." Then, "Cupid's dart" and "My poor heart" made a very pretty rhyme. As a little relief, *art* was sometimes ingeniously used with either heart or dart. But whatever the combination it must be said that the result was very bad art, mangled heart, and pointless dart; but what matter so long as the "beautious fair" was touched, and consented to be her admirer's valentine for life?

When those useful little books of verses came out, then was valentine writing made easy for even the most unpoetical; and cobblers, butchers, bakers, and shoemakers could make use of trade terms to advantage. Here are some specimens taken from an old book printed in England in 1812, called the " Cabinet of Love; or, Cupid's Repository of Choice Valentines."

This is for a young lady who evidently thinks it the twenty-ninth instead of the fourteenth of February, as she is proposing in true leap year fashion:

> " Kind youth, allow a youthful maid
>   To send these trembling lines,
>   And speak the secrets of her heart
>   On day of Valentine.
>   Long has she felt Love's tender flame,
>   And long the same concealed;
>   Trusting, by time or fortune's aid,
>   That flame might be revealed.

And oh! how happy I would be
If freed my heart from pain,
And for my heart you would, in truth,
Return me yours again."

From a baker:

"In these hard times it truly may be said
That half a loaf's much better than no bread;
Then surely, pretty dear, you glad may be
Since sure of loaves enough, to marry me."

From a butcher:

"My nice little lamb,
Your lover I am;
I've money and got a good trade.
My shop it is neat,
My house is complete:
All ready for you, my sweet maid.

"On dainties so fine
Each day we will dine
And act as you please, your will shall
    be mine.
So your answer I pray,
And hope you'll say aye,
And bless with your heart your true
                    Valentine."

This is for those who like the play of *heart, dart,* and *dart, heart:*

> "Dear girl, I'm up to ears in love!
> The fact a thousand follies prove:
>   Yes, yes, I feel the dart.
> Well, now I'm wounded, give the cure,
> Thou'rt not a cruel girl, I'm sure,
>   So try to ease my heart.
>
> "O, far from me those lightnings dart:
>   On others bid thy beauty shine;
> Beyond the hopes of this sad heart
>   I view that peerless form to pine."

The thought is somewhat confused, but the rhyme is there, and would do for a young lady who was in no way critical.

Here we have the variation of *art* and *heart,* in the lines to a coquette:

> "Whilst ev'ry shepherd sings her praise,
>   'Tis mine of Betsy to complain:
> Made a poor pris'ner while I gaze,
>   I feel in ev'ry smile a chain.
>
> "And are you then a thing of art,
>   Seducing all and loving none?
> And have I strove to gain a heart
>   Which ev'ry shepherd thinks his own?"

This form for a shoemaker's valentine is given with its answer:

> "A piece of charming kid you are
>   As e'er mine eyes did see,
> No calf-skin smooth that e'er I saw
>   Can be compared with thee.
>
> "You are my all, do not refuse
>   To let us tack together;
> But let us join, my Valentine,
>   Like sole and upper leather.

"ANSWER

> "My merry friend,
>   You've gained your end;
>   My heart is truly thine:
> I do not choose
> For to refuse
>   A constant Valentine."

This seems unfair to the young lady, who might decline to accept the cobbler; there should have been a verse for her. Now she must refuse to answer, resort to plain prose, or accept him in spite of herself, by using the prepared answer because there is no other.

The use of these little manuals was necessarily short-lived. They served a purpose for a time, then people looked about for something more original.

For many years after the manufactured valentine came into vogue, valentine sending was at its height. Everybody could have one for a price, from the plain little sheet, with its wood-cut and single sentiment, to wonderfully frilled and furbelowed lace paper affairs, which unfolded many times, with a fresh love-message surprising you at every turn.

There was no necessity for the simple, home-made expressions of esteem; yet, in those gaudy machine-made ones, was lost that bit of personal essence which must have been infused into those made by the young men and maidens who had so much of themselves to express.

What comparison could possibly be drawn between these ready-to-wear kind, and the

St. Valentine's Day

SAM WELLER INDITING HIS VALENTINE

heartfelt emotions so laboriously expressed by the immortal Sam Weller, written on a sheet of gilt-edge letter-paper, with a hard-nibbed pen warranted not to splutter. Dickens portrays his painstaking efforts very vividly, as he draws up the table in front of the fire, spreads his paper out carefully, squares his elbows, dips the pen in the ink, and prepares to pour out the sentiments of his soul to Mary, Housemaid at Mr. Nupkin's, Mayor's, Ipswich, Suffolk. The appearance on the scene, an hour and a half later, of the elder Mr. Weller, somewhat embarrassed poor " Samivel," but he explained that he was writing a " walentine," and offered to read it. Weller, Sr., admitted to being horrified, but under the soothing influence of his pipe, ordered his son to "fire away." Thus encouraged, this is what he read, supplemented with many suggestions and corrections from his parent; and a good bit of hard studying to make out his own intentions through the numerous blots ::

"Lovely —"

This was more than his father could stand without some stimulant, so the waiting-maid was called and received the order, " A double glass o' the inwariable, my dear." Again Sam began, with a very theatrical air:

" Lovely creetur i feel myself ashamed and completely circumscribed in a dressin' of you, for you are a nice gal and nothin' but it," which having been approved by his parent as " a wery pretty sentiment," Sam continued:

" Afore I see you I thought all women was alike, but now I find what a reg'lar soft-headed inkred'lous turnip I must ha' been, for there ain't nobody like you though I like you better than nothin' at all."

Sam stopped long enough to remark that he thought best to make that rather strong, and, having received a nod of approval, re-sumed:

"So I take the privilidge of the day, Mary my dear, as the gen'l'm'n in difficulties did wen he walked out of a Sunday, to tell you that the first and only time I see you, your likeness was took on my heart in much quicker time and brighter colors than ever a likeness was. took by the profeel macheen (wich p'r'aps you may have heard on, Mary my dear), altho' it *does* finish a portrait and put the frame and glass on complete with a hook at the end to hang it up by, and all in two seconds and a quarter.

"Except of me, Mary my dear, as your walentine, and think over what I've said. My dear Mary, I will now conclude," and after much controversy over what the sig-nature should be, he compromised by signing himself "Your love sick, Pickwick."

It is strange that a day so distinctly marked in its character should have so vague an origin. Archbishop Wheatly connects the celebration of the day directly with St. Valentine, and says that " he was a man of most admirable parts, and was so famous for his love and charity that the custom of choosing valentines upon his festival took its form from thence." Another says that the martyred priest of Rome seems to have had nothing at all to do with the matter of observances which originated in obscurity like many other ceremonial days. Yet another speaks of St. Valentine as an austere saint, and cannot reconcile the festive observance of this day with such a character. Some other one, who seems to know all about it, has given us a story of the banishment of the saint and his connection with St. Valentine's Day.

There ruled in the palace at Rome the Emperor Claudius. He was called Claudius the Cruel. Near the palace, in a great Greek temple, there stood a high priest. This priest, whose name was Valentine, was popular with the whole city, and so great was his popularity that his church was crowded, and around the altars and fires knelt all the wise people of Rome. Plebeians and patricians, young and old, rich and poor, ignorant and wise, all went to learn of Valentine and be blessed by him.

In the midst of this popularity there arose wars outside of Rome, and the emperor called his citizens forth to battle.

But the wars continued year after year, and many were loath to go. The married ones did not want to leave their families, and those who were engaged to be married openly demurred at the thought of going away from their sweethearts.

On hearing this the emperor became very angry, and sent forth a decree that, from that time on, there should be no more marriages. Not only should there be no weddings, but those who were engaged to be married should break their engagements.

At this the young girls died of love, and the young men went to their work by day with a moody expression of countenance and with heavy hearts. Of what use to draw water and hew stone, and bake the vases in the potteries, if there could be no marriages?

When the good-priest Valentine heard of this he was very sad. One day, quite secretly, he united a couple standing under the sacred altars. Then others came to him, and quietly he wedded them. And still others, and others, until the marriage business in old Rome was as good as it was before the decree went forth forbidding all weddings.

At last the news reached the palace, and the emperor, hearing it, was exceedingly wroth. " Go take that man Valentine," said he, " and cast him into a dungeon. I will have no man in Rome who refuses to obey my commands."

The emperor's counsellors pleaded with him in vain. "Be careful," said they, "for Valentine has many and powerful friends, and there may be trouble if they should rise up against you."

But Claudius would not listen, and Valentine was dragged from the altar while in the very act of uniting a couple, and taken to prison.

There he languished and died, for not all the efforts of his friends could free him.

But each year, on the anniversary of his birth, the people met and honored his name. They talked about him, his life, his work, and his good deeds. Many were married on this night, for they said: "In that way we shall best keep his memory green." This is a very pretty theory, and appeals to those who like to have the origin in keeping with the celebration of the day; but the probable origin of St. Valentine's Day is the ancient feast in honor of Pan and Juno, held by the early Romans during the month of February.

The Christian leaders persuaded their converts to allow them to substitute St. Valentine for pagan Pan and Juno, and the date of the saint's death, the fourteenth of February, as the day of celebration.

The new name and date did not disturb the people so long as the festivities remained the same, and until a few years ago the sentiment, though changing its expression according to the age and nationality of the people, was as strong as in the early Christian times.

A favorite St. Valentine custom of two hundred years ago was the drawing from a kind of lottery, when the names of the young men and women of the company were taken from a box. The maiden whose name was drawn, was to be the valentine of the young man who drew it for that day.

Sometimes they remained each other's

valentine for life, for there was a certain superstitious regard for this chance selection; and though not altogether binding, every influence of association tended to make it so. Whoever was first looked upon by one of the opposite sex, was considered bound, for the day, at least, to be that person's valentine, and all the superstitions of the age helped on the cause of real and would-be lovers.

Gay tells us of one country maiden whose head was filled with this idea, yet she did not neglect her milking:

> "Last Valentine, the day when birds of kind
> Their paramours with mutual chirpings find,
> I early rose, just at the break of day,
> Before the sun had chased the stars away;
> Afield I went, amid the morning dew,
> To milk my kine (for so should housewives do).
> Thee first I spied — and the first swain we see
> In spite of Fortune shall our true love be."

Another young lady thought it no sin to help fortune in favoring her, for in an old magazine of more than a hundred years ago, *The Connoisseur,* of 1754, we find this confession of heroic self-mortification.

"Last Friday was St. Valentine's Day, and the night before I got five bay leaves and pinned four on the corners of my pillow, and the fifth to the middle; and then if I dreamt of my sweetheart, Betty said we should be married before the year was out. But to make it more sure I boiled an egg hard and took out the yolk and filled it with salt; and when I went to bed ate it shell and all, without speaking or drinking after it. We also wrote our lovers' names upon bits of paper, and rolled them up in clay and put them into water; and the first that rose up was to be our valentine. Would you think it? Mr. Blossom was my man. I lay abed and shut my eyes all the morning, till he came to our house, for I would not have seen another man before him for all the world."

In Western Europe there is a custom for the fourteenth of February, when it is considered not indelicate for a maiden to pay addresses to any man whom she might particularly favor.

It is quite certain that these Valentine's Day ceremonies, pointing so obviously to one result, existed in those days when all the daughters of the family were supposed to marry, and no other career was even thought of.

It was quite possible and well understood that one must take advantage of all the favors which St. Valentine had to bestow, for did he not hold the fate of lovers in his hand?

Mr. Pepys writes in his diary on St. Valentine's Day in 1667: " This morning came up to my wife's bedside little Will Mercer to be her valentine, and brought her name written upon blue paper in gold letters, done by himself, very pretty; and we were both well pleased with it. But I am also this year my wife's valentine; and it will cost me five pounds; but that I must have laid out if we had not been valentines." On another fourteenth of February he writes: "Up, being called up by Mercer, who came to be my valentine, and I did give her a guinny in gold for her valentine gift.

" There comes Roger Pepys betimes, and comes to my wife, for her to be his valentine. I was also, by agreement; and this year I find it is likely to cost four or five pounds in a ring for her, which she desires."

From this little glimpse into his private life, we see that for Mr. Pepys, St. Valentine's Day was not without its financial burden, though he seems to have met his obligations cheerfully.

In the essays of Elia, Charles Lamb touches this day of universal love in his delicately humorous way:

" Hail to thy returning festival, old Bishop

Valentine! Great immortal go-between! Who and what manner of person art thou?

"Art thou but a name typifying the restless principle, which impels poor humans to seek perfection in union? or wert thou indeed a mortal prelate with thy tippet and thy apron on, and decent lawn sleeves?

"Mysterious personage! like unto thee, assuredly there was no other mitred father in the calendar. Thou comest attended with thousands and tens of thousands of little loves, and the air is ' Brushed with the kiss of nestling wings.'

"This is the day on which those charming little missives called valentines cross and intercross each other at every turning.

"Not many sounds in life exceed in interest the knock at the door. It 'gives a very echo to the throne where Hope is seated.' But its issues seldom answer to this oracle within. It is seldom that just the person we want to see comes. But of all the clamorous visitations, the welcomest in expectation is the sound that ushers in a valentine.

" When letters cease to be written (but not till then), when love shall be no more — then shall this amorous and holy-day darken and grow common; then shall it be a mere vulgar root (now how full of rare and sweet flowers!) in the wilderness of days — a garden in the deserts of time. Valentines pervade all space, like light."

However we may observe the day of St. Valentine, its character has been stamped by the generations who entered into its celebration sincerely, joyously, spontaneously; and however indifferent we may be, we cannot escape that influence which is the inheritance of years gone by, when swains became gallants, and the humblest maiden was made happy with a devoted valentine for at least a day.

If we do not resort to the simple primitive expressions of our fancy used by our forefathers, we certainly have sentiments to express which we may do as delicately as we choose; and it will do us no harm to partake of the old-time fragrance, though we celebrate only with musing on what has been.

Yet, in spite of the hopeful prophecy of Elia, it is true that now, almost everywhere, St. Valentine's Day is (outwardly, at least) a much degenerated festival. Though it still has its fascination for children and a few older people, it cannot be said that the day is honored with much celebration. Those highly colored caricatures and burlesque verses, miscalled comic valentines, which carry hideousness and unkindness, are not to be considered for a moment in the St. Valentine idea of loving thought, truthfully expressed. These so-called valentines are a product of modern commercialism without regard for sentiment or legend, and are sent only by those who fail to grasp even a shadow of the real meaning and intention of this saint's day.

Elia said, " I love to keep all festivals, to taste all feast offerings," and he entered into the full thought and spirit of the occasion when he wrote his first valentine, which was certainly written with no other idea than to give pleasure, and is dedicated to that " fair siren with a low, melodious voice."

"Why is the rose of the East so fond
  Of the bird on the near palm-tree?
  'Tis because he sings like the murmurings
  Of the river that runs so bright and free.

"And why doth the paradise creature sing
  To the silent and clear blue air,
  When many a sound from the woods around
  Doth speak like a spell to entice him there?

"'Tis because the blush of his love is rich,
  And richer grow his glances gay:
  'Tis because the flower which fills the hour
  With beauty, would pine were he away.

"Yet what is the red of the rose to thine?
  And what is the nightingale's soft love-eye?

Thy glance is as bright as the clear star light
And the blush of thy cheek hath a deeper dye.

" Therefore, and because of thy reed-rich song
   May vie with the best of the Muses mine,
   Do I, a poet (though none may know it),
   Choose *thee,* fair girl, for my Valentine."

ALL FOOLS' DAY

ALL FOOLS' DAY

"I must have liberty
Withal, as large a charter as the wind,
To blow on whom I please; for so fools have;
And they that are most galled with my folly,
They most must laugh. And why, sir, must they so?
The 'why' is plain as way to parish church:
He that a fool doth very wisely hit
Doth very foolishly, although he smart,
Not to seem senseless of the bob: if not,
The wise man's folly is anatomized
Even by the squandering glances of the fool."
                                        —*As You Like It.*

"Wit, and it be thy will, put me into good fooling!
Those that think they have thee, do very oft prove
fools; and I, that am sure I lack thee, may pass
for a wise man: For what says Quinapalus? Better
a witty fool than a foolish wit."
                                        — *Twelfth Night.*

"Nay, I'll come; if I lose a scruple of this sport,
let me be boiled to death with melancholy."
                                        — *Twelfth Night.*

"The more pity, that fools may not speak wisely
what wise men do foolishly."
                                        —*As You Like It.*

ALL FOOLS' DAY

" Mr. ——, you look wise. Pray correct that error."
                                    — ELIA.
        " I confess
I am not very wise, and yet I find
A fool, so be he parcel knave, in court
May flourish and grow rich."
                    — MASSINGER's *Calandrino*.

WHAT man is there who would not rather commit sin than to appear ridiculous in the eyes of his neighbors, or what man through an uncomfortable memory makes himself more unhappy than he who has been fooled by another?

Deception may be varied to touch every chord in human nature, and the whole gamut of sensibility may be easily played upon, if one skilfully understands the art of fooling.

From the days of Eden, when the devil outwitted Eve, and Eve deluded Adam, to the present-day schoolboy who pins a placard inscribed " Kick me " on the coat-tails of his conscientious teacher, the ingenuity of the race has ever been active in inventing new methods by which one man could successfully fool his brother.

Whether by slow, premeditated planning, carefully worked out, or by spontaneous mirth-creating methods, the practice is forever carried on.

Some one has been bold enough to say that people like to be deceived; and there is usually some accommodating person ready to oblige the public. If he is shrewd enough to succeed in pleasing, no matter how grave the hoax, he is considered a clever fellow, and his deception is excused. Should he happen to strike the wrong chord, or if his chord be slightly out of tune with the popular ear, he is then simply called an ignominious fellow, and should be put into jail.

The typical fool is the merry fool, the mirth-creating, laughing fool; and one who can fool others and at the same time provoke no resentment. All men are born with some sense of humor as they are born with a conscience; and the man who cannot laugh is as much a moral monstrosity as one whose conscience is so latent as to be invisible.

How highly mirth was esteemed in very ancient times is shown by Lycurgus, who raised an image of Laughter and caused it to be worshipped as a god. " He loved," he said, " to see people merry."

Even as early as the fifth century before the Christian era, people understood the necessity of being amused, and making fun had become a profession. We have the epi-taph of a heathen jester whose wit was evidently not of the most wholesome kind: " Having drunk much, eaten much, and

L. of C.

spoken much evil, here I lie, Timocreon of Rhodes."

So the fool, ancient and modern, the professional, the self-made, and occasional fool, is and has always been, everywhere present. That a day should have been set apart for their especial honor seems reasonable enough since, as Dickens said, " They are so numerous, and fill so many positions of dignity and importance; " but why the first of April was chosen as the Feast of Fools no one seems to know.

Antiquarians have puzzled themselves and others with attempts to account for the custom of fool-making, but their researches have established nothing except that the practice is very ancient and very general.

Some of the theories advanced by serious men of learning would make even a fool think. It must have been an April fool who said that his day was established by Noah, who made the mistake of sending out the dove; and to send a person upon a *sleeveless errand* simply follows the example of the patriarch who sent the bird on a useless message.

Another ingenious person says that perhaps *All Fools'* is derived from that transaction between the Romans and Sabines. The Roman soldiers during the infancy of their city wanted wives, and finding that they could not obtain the neighboring women by peaceable addresses, resolved to make use of strategy. Accordingly, the Romans instituted certain games to be performed on the first of April, in honor of Neptune. Upon hearing of this, the bordering inhabitants with their whole families flocked to Rome to see the mighty celebration, and thereupon the Romans seized a great number of the Sabine women for wives. This theory is not a pleasant one, and we refuse to tolerate a brutal practical joke as the origin of the day, as we do in its annual celebration.

Some one, not satisfied with existing theories, propounded a new one, which places the origin of All Fools' Day for England among the ancient Britons, at the " Festum Fatuorum." The early Christians, in order to attract the pagans to a better worship, humored their prejudices by yielding to their customs, when they did not interfere with the fundamental gospel doctrines. This proved an excellent method to prevent the people from returning to their old religion.

At this feast, part of the jollity of the season was a burlesque election of mock pope, mock cardinals and bishops, attended with a thousand ridiculous ceremonies, gambols, and antics, grotesque attitudes, and singing of ludicrous anthems.

All the ceremonies intentionally alluded to the exploded pretensions of the Druids, whom these sports were calculated to expose to scorn and derision. This Feast of Fools had its designed effect, and contributed more

All Fools' Day

Village Frolic on April
First

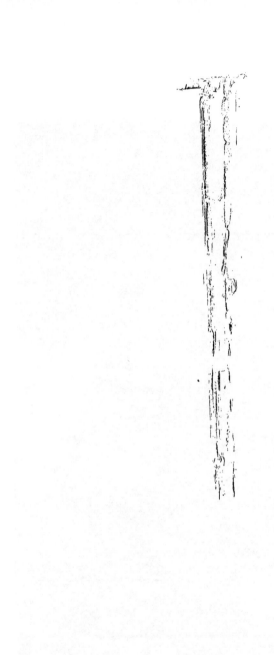

toward the extermination of the heathen beliefs than the combined force of fire and sword, both of which were unsparingly used in the persecution of those who held them.

The Romans had a similar feast, as we learn from Plutarch, who asks: "Why do they call the Quirinalia the Feast of Fools?" He then answers himself by saying: "Either because they allowed this day (as Juba tells us) to those who could not ascertain their own tribes, or because they had permitted those who had missed the celebration of the Formacalia in their proper tribes along with the rest of the people, either from business, absence, or ignorance, to hold their festival apart on this day."

So evidently this celebration among the Romans was instituted for the unfortunate ones who had missed the pleasures of the great national feast held earlier in the season.

In various parts of Europe a day of fools is observed, and among the Hindus, fool-making is in full force at their celebration of the Huli festival, which is kept the thirty-first of March. This is one of the most ancient of Hindu celebrations, and high and low join in it. Even those of the highest rank take delight in making Huli fools, and carry a joke so far as to send letters, making appointments in the names of persons known to be away from home on a certain date.

And so we find that in nearly all parts of the earth there exists a day which corresponds to our All Fools', and though there has been a great display of learning, and many theories upon the subject, there is no satisfactory or even plausible conclusion as to the origin of this day. We must therefore accept without much questioning this rhyme found in Poor Robin's Almanack for 1760, —

> "The first of April, some do say,
> Is set apart for All Fools' Day;
> But why the people call it so
> Nor I, nor they themselves, do know," —

and believe that according to existing conditions it was necessary to appoint a day
for the general hoaxing of man by mankind.

When we consider the divine origin of
fools, it is not surprising that they should
be thought worthy of all honor. An old
legend tells us that fools were made by the
gods, and were the product of necessity.

It is said that Zeus found Olympus exceedingly dull, and complained that among
all the gods there was not one fool
with wit enough to keep the rest cheerful.
" Father," said Mercury, " the diversion may
be found for us on earth; for look! do
you not see that crowd of folk in holiday
gear, dancing, singing, and eating? I think
it would be great sport to send a shower to
spoil their finery." " Thy thought is witless
as it stands," said the Olympian, " but it
may be improved. Let that serene priest
below tell the people that a shower is about
to descend, but that it shall wet only fools."

The sound of thunder aroused the priest, who made the required announcement to the people. A philosopher, leaning against his door-post, on hearing it, withdrew and shut himself into his study, but not another person prepared to avoid the storm. Each man waited to see the *fools* drenched, and so every man was wet to the skin. When the sun shone, the philosopher sauntered into the market-place, while the soaked ones hailed him with " Fool." They pelted him with stones, tore his gown, plucked his beard, and loaded him with vile tongue-twisting terms. But the wise philosopher said to the crowd: " Wait for a single minute, and I will prove to you that I am not such a fool as I look; " and, casting his eyes skyward, he said: " O wise father of the witty and the witless, send down upon me a deluge; wet me to the skin even as these fools are wet; make me as great a fool as my neighbors, and help me, in consequence of being a fool, to live at peace among fools." The shower fell, and the dripping sage rose from his knees wittier than before. This request with its result so pleased Jupiter that he said to his attendant divinities: "Children, let us drink to him. Here's a health to the first of fools!" And since that time folly has never left the earth.

A later version of the story adds that the sage fool was rewarded for his sagacity by being appointed jester at the court of a great king, and that he was the father of all the fools, who for centuries were important members of the royal courts. These clever fellows were always useful and ever welcome, especially if their kings happened to be particularly stupid ones. If the jester caused laughter the royal master would stroke his beard, and modestly smile, as though he himself had said the good things uttered by his fool.

It was the privilege of the professional all-the-year-round fool to exercise very great license of speech, and many unpleasant truths have been told to tyrants who would have punished the speaker with death had he been a courtier. Kings of all times have been amused by their jesters, even with jokes at their own expense; but occasionally the royal patron was in no mood to hear free speech, and sometimes a poor fool lost his head for an untimely jest. But usually nothing the jester might say, whatever he might mean, was ever taken as serious. "There is no slander," says Olivia in Twelfth Night, "in an allowed fool;" and the clown also defines his own standing when he says: "I am not her fool, but her corrupter of words."

Viola portrays all that a fool should be in the words:

"This fellow's wise enough to play the fool;
And to do that well craves a kind of wit:

He must observe their mood on whom he jests,
The quality of persons and the time;
And like the haggard, check at every feather
That comes before his eye. This is a practice,
As full of labor as a wise man's art:
For folly, that he wisely shows, is fit;
But wise men, folly fallen, taint their wit."

Like the fools of later years, these jesters have served to kill time for their dull companions. When society was without books, and supported a class of idle, aimless nobles, it learned what it could, and amused itself as it might with the help of fools, dwarfs, and jesters.

The progress of modern times has killed neither mirth, jests, nor jesters, but it has given every man the right and ability to be his own fool. Why, then, should we not have at least one day in the calendar in which to exercise our particular capabilities in the direction of fool-making?

What would this man have done had he not been given the opportunity to add his splendid contribution each year? "A neighbor of mine," says the Spectator, " who is a haberdasher by trade, and a very shallow and conceited fellow, makes his boasts that for ten years successively he has made not less than a hundred fools." This is truly an incredible record.

The English Earl of Orford has said of April Fools' Day: " The oldest tradition affirms that such an infatuation attends the first day of April as no foresight can escape, no vigilance can defeat. Deceit is successful that day out of the mouths of babes and sucklings. Grave citizens have been bit upon it; usurers have lent money on bad security; experienced matrons have married very disappointed young fellows; mathematicians have missed the longitude; alchymists the philosophers' stone; and politicians preferment on that day. What confusion will not follow if the great body of the nation are disappointed of their peculiar holiday!"

Under the cloak of folly a good turn has been rendered to wise men, and kings are sometimes fooled by those who are not court jesters. By feigning want of wit, the Wise Men of Gotham favored themselves and completely hoodwinked their king. King John of England, so the story is told, was marching toward Nottingham intending to pass through Gotham meadow. The villagers believed that the ground over which a king passed became, forever after, a public road; and not being minded to part with their meadow so cheaply, they caused the king to be led around another way. Enraged at their incivility, he sent to inquire into their rudeness, intending to punish them severely. These wise men, on hearing that messengers were coming from the king, decided to save themselves by fooling the king again, by making fools of themselves. When the king's servants arrived they found some of the inhabitants trying to drown an eel

in a pond; some dragging a cart to the top
of a barn to protect it from the sun's rays;
some rolling cheeses down-hill, expecting
that they would find their way to Nottingham market, and some trying to hedge in a
cuckoo which had perched upon a bush.

They were all at work at such foolish
capers that the king's officers decided that
it was a village of fools, and consequently
unworthy of his Majesty's notice. Some
skeptical poet has written his opinion of this
thirteenth-century story:

> "Tell me no more of Gotham fools,
>   Or of their eels in little pools,
>   Which they, we're told, were drowning:
>   Nor of their carts drawn up on high
>   When King John's men were standing by,
>   To keep the wood from browning.

> "Nor of their cheese shoved down the hill,
>   Nor of the cuckoo sitting still,
>   While it they hedged around;
>   Such tales of them have long been told,
>   By prating boobies young and old,
>   In drunken circles crowned.

"The fools are those who thither go,
　To see the cuckoo bush, I trow,
　　The wood, the barn, the pools;
For such are seen both here and there,
And passèd by without a sneer,
　　By all but errant fools."

The April Fool idea is so strong in some countries that only a bold man would start an enterprise on the first of April; and to be married on that day would bring down all sorts of jeers on the heads of the courageous couple. To be sure, Napoleon I. and Maria Louisa were married on All Fools' Day, but we know that Napoleon was not to be hindered in his plans by any ordinary obstacle; and his knowledge of French ridicule and the probable ill-natured jokes of Parisian farçeurs had no effect.

It is said that the Duke of Lorraine, with his wife, made their escape while the French officers were enjoying an April fool. The duke and duchess, who had been in captivity at Nantes, disguised themselves as peasants:

one holding a hod on his shoulder, and the other carrying a basket of rubbish on her back, they passed through the gates of the city at an early hour. A woman, thinking that she recognized the persons, ran to a guard to give notice to the sentry, but the soldier cried, " April fool! " The governor, to whom the story was told as a jest, was suspicious, and ordered the fact to be proved. But by this time it was too late, as the duke and duchess were far out of reach. However successful this attempt may have been, it is not always best to try to fool those in authority. It is better even to avoid the appearance of trying. A French lady was accused of stealing a watch, but she persistently denied the charge, saying that it could not be found among her possessions, and urged that some one might be sent to search for it. The officer, being an obliging man, sent a subordinate, who found the property and brought it to the magistrate; but the lady, remembering that it was the first of April, laughed long and loudly, and said: "This is a rare joke. What excellent April fools you all are!" The dull officer failed to see the joke, but thought that somehow the lady was the April fool, and felt sure that such as she had better be confined; so he sent her to jail till the next first of April, thinking that a year of meditation might teach her to suit her jokes to her company.

The Scotch, who dearly love a practical joke, are not content with a simple fool. There must be complications, and the laugh is always in proportion to the trouble given. They delight to send a neighbor, not upon a single *sleeveless* errand, but as many as he will before finding out that he is being hoaxed. Some one sends simple Sandy to a neighbor a couple of miles away, with a note containing the words:

> "This is the first of April;
> Hunt the gowk another mile."

The waggish neighbor says to Sandy: " I cannot supply my friend with the hoe he wants, but you will find one at neighbor MacGowan's." So off goes Sandy a mile beyond to MacGowan, who, being also a wag, sends him to a third neighbor for the imaginary hoe. It is always reasoned that the number of miles travelled by Sandy that day depends solely upon how much of a fool he is; and a successful affair of this kind will keep the rustics in fun for a week; and Sandy's spirits will be made very heavy. Sandy may not have been a fool at all; only a simple confiding gowk, who, with bitter results, has accommodated his neighbors.

To make a successful April fool there must be nothing malicious, nor should there be made a definite or false assertion. To state positively that there is a great hole in the back of a man's coat is no joke, but a lie; but by dexterous suggestion you must modestly hint, for his own good, of course, that there are several little holes in his coat. The man is horrified (he has just called upon his fiancée), and when he cries, "What! where? Bramble-bush, barbed-wire!" you quietly say, "Buttonholes," and wonder if it is really necessary to add, "April fool!"

The old-fashioned schoolboy tricks were good in this respect. You were sent to the cobbler's shop for strap-oil; you were not told anything as to the nature of the article, neither was it positively stated that the cobbler really sold it. If your reason did not lead you to make inquiries as to a cobbler's stock in trade, or if you had not taken the trouble to find out the day of the month, you were richly rewarded by a strapping which the jolly cobbler was privileged to give.

Then it should have been clear to even the simple-minded that on the first of April "gander ile" was not an article of commerce. If it did not occur to you to ask for goose oil, which every croupy boy knew, you must certainly be regarded as an April fool.

There is some little satisfaction when a boy has successfully fooled his playmate, but his fullest delight is not reached till he has brought his superior in position and intellect to feel how painful and degrading is the position of an April fool. No man really likes a joke at his own expense, even when it happens to be a good one; but to be sold in the presence of others, by young gamins who, with exultant whoops of triumph, have fled before you, gives a man a shock that remains with him the rest of the day. He has the feeling that he is branded with the words " April fool " in thirty-six line type; everybody must see it, and no intellectual superiority, or contempt for the first of April with its vulgar practices, will avail him.

The spirit of the day touches all, young

All Fools'

"THE APRIL F

and old, in high or low station. In the Bairnsla Foak Annual for 1844, some gowk says: "Ah think ah needant tell you at this iz April-fooil Day, cos, if yor like me, yol naw all abaght it, for ah wonce sent a this day to a stationer's shop for't seckand edishan a Cock Robin, an a haupath a crockadile quills; Ah thowt fasure, at when ah axt for am, at chap it shop ad a splittin t' caanter stop we' laffin."

Goldsmith, in the "Vicar of Wakefield," describing the manners of some rustics, tells us that among other customs which they followed they "showed their wit on the first of April." This surely could not have been in the locality of Bairnsla.

We know that even Dean Swift did not let All Fools' Day pass unnoticed, for, in his "Journal to Stella," he enters under March thirty-first, 1713, that he, Doctor Arbuthnot, and Lady Masham had been amusing themselves that evening by "contriving a lie for to-morrow."

Elia, writing on the first of April, has given us a humorous touch quite in sympathy with what the spirit of All Fools' should be. After many witty flights, he says: "To descend and not to protract our Fools banquet — for I think the second of April is not many hours distant — in sober verity I will confess a truth to thee, reader. I love a Fool as naturally as if I were kith and kin to him. When a child I read those Parables, not guessing their involved wisdom. I had more yearnings towards that simple architect that built his house on the sand, than I entertained for his more cautious neighbor; I grudged the hard censure pronounced upon the quiet soul that kept his talent; and, prizing their simplicity beyond the more provident, and, to my apprehension, somewhat *unfeminine* wariness of their competitors, I felt a kindliness that

almost amounted to *tendre* for those five
thoughtless virgins.

"I venerate an honest obliquity of under-
standing. The more laughable blunders a
man shall commit in your company, the more
tests that he will not betray or overreach
you. And take my word for this, reader,
and say a fool told you, if you please, that
he who hath not a dram of folly in his
mixture hath pounds of worse matter in his
composition.

"It is said, 'The foolisher the fowl or
fish the finer the flesh thereof,' and what are
commonly called the world's received fools
but such whereof the world is not worthy?
And what have been some of the kindliest
patterns of our species but so many darlings
of absurdity?

"Reader, if you invest my words beyond
their fair construction, it is you and not I
that are the April Fool."

An English rhymester has shown us the principal features of an old-time Fools' Day:

"On this great day are people sent
On purpose for pure merriment;
And though the day is known before,
Yet frequently there is great store
Of those forgetfuls to be found,
Who're sent to dance Moll Dixon's round;
And having tried each shop and stall,
And disappointed at them all,
At last some tells them of the cheat,
Then they return from the pursuit,
And straightway home with shame they run,
While others laugh at what is done.
But 'tis a thing to be disputed,
Which is the greatest fool reputed,
The man that innocently went,
Or he that him design'dly sent."

So long-lived are customs attached to particular days that it is very probable that April Fools' Day will survive through many generations; and as the delights of fooling are perennial, so long as man lives, there will be attendant fools.

EASTER

"In the bonds of Death He lay,
　　Who for our offence was slain;
But the Lord is risen to-day,
　　Christ hath brought us life again.
Wherefore let us all rejoice,
Singing loud with cheerful voice
　　　　　　　　Hallelujah!

. . . .

"Let us keep high festival
　　On this most blessed day of days,
When God His mercy showed to all;
　　Our Sun is risen with brightest rays,
And our dark hearts rejoice to see
Sin and Night before Him flee.
　　　　　　　　Hallelujah!

"To the supper of the Lord,
　　Gladly will we come to-day;
The word of peace is now restored,
　　The old leaven is put away.
Christ will be our food alone,
Faith no life but His doth own.
　　　　　　　　Hallelujah!"
　　　　　　　—LUTHER'S *Easter Hymn.*

EASTER

"We know that this Easter Day shines on a nobler world than that of a century ago. We know that that Easter was brighter than that of a century before. We know that our children's children a century hence will look back on the Christian civilization of to-day, amazed, indeed, that we should think it worthy of congratulation."

— E. E. HALE.

"Because He lived, this world begins to live to-day. And of its Spiritual birth this day is the anniversary."

— E. E. HALE.

EASTER SUNDAY was formerly called the "Sunday of Joy," and, like many other festival days, which have come down to us from earlier times, has been changed from its original character to a religious observance, and is now the festival of the resurrection of our Lord.

We know that long ago, there was a feast of the Teutonic goddess Ostèra, who was the personification of the East, of the Morning, and of Spring. The Anglo-Saxon name was Eastre — from which, naturally enough, comes our Easter — and the month of April, which was dedicated to her, was called Eastermonath; it is still known in Germany as " Ostermonat."

The worship of Ostera was deeply rooted in northèrn Germany, and was brought into England by the Saxons; and the early missionaries, finding it impossible to abolish it, endeavored, as they had done in so many other cases, to change it to a Christian festival and to give to it a religious significance. This was more easily done than in some other instances; for the joy at the climbing sun, the lengthening day, the bursting of spring from the clutch of winter, and the universal resurrection of natural things, could quite easily be changed in thought

to joy at the rising of the Sun of Right-
eousness, the power of Christ over death,
and his release from the grave.

Although the Church has always been
united as to why Easter should be celebrated,
there has been a wide difference of opinion
as to when it should be observed.

The first Christians retained many of the
Mosaic customs, though later they were altogether abolished or held as only typical of
some occurrence in the Christian religion;
and the festival of Easter took its origin
from the feast of the Passover, kept by the
Jews on the fourteenth day of Nisan — the
Hebrew month corresponding to our March
or April, and the Eastern Church observed
that date, while the Western Church, remembering that Christ rose on Sunday, had its
festival on the Sunday following the day
celebrated by the Jews and Eastern Christians. The discussion as to the true date
was kept up until the time of Constantine,

who, in 325, brought the subject before the
Council at Nice, and from that time Easter
Sunday has been everywhere on one and
the same day, — the first Sunday after the
full moon which comes upon, or next after,
the twenty-first of March. If the full moon
occurs upon Sunday, Easter Day is the following Sunday.

One would think this an easy and infallible rule, for there must always be a moon,
and it is pretty sure to be full, sometime
during the month; but even in following the
moon there is difficulty, for these Church
authorities decided to regulate the time of
Easter, not by the actual moon, nor what is
called by astronomers the " mean moon,"
but by an imaginary, ecclesiastical moon,
whose movements follow the real moon by
two or three days. However, this dog-
matic moon serves its purpose, and may be
depended upon, so long as it lags behind

the other regularly, and keeps in the same relation to it.

The Easter festival in very early days was introduced by fasting on one day only — the Friday before, known as Good Friday — and the night preceding was devoted to prayer and thanksgiving until the time of cock-crow, which the people believed to be the moment of Christ's resurrection. Later the fast was extended to forty hours, the length of time that Christ lay in the tomb; and afterwards the period of preparation was prolonged to forty days, — the season of temptation in the Wilderness.

The early Christians, on Easter morning, greeted each other with " Christ is risen," to which the person addressed answered, " Christ hath risen indeed, and hath appeared to Simon."

All the ceremonies attending the observance of Easter were at first exceedingly simple; but in the early part of the fourth century, a decided change was brought about. Constantine, who, it is said, was fond of display, showed his love of parade by celebrating this festival with extraordinary pomp. Night-watches were instituted in the churches until midnight; the tapers which had been used at this time were not thought sufficient, so huge pillars of wax were used instead. Not only were they placed in the churches, but all over the city, so that people might be tricked into thinking that the flames of Constantine's night-candles far exceeded the sunlight. Easter Sunday was filled with most elaborate ceremonials, the Pope officiating at mass, with the most imposing service that could be devised.

Various ceremonies, sports, and superstitions have in times past characterized the day, and still many of the old Easter customs are practised in different parts of the world.

The days preceding Easter were observed

in various ways, secular and otherwise. In England, Good Friday and hot-cross buns are synonymous. The bun seems to be an institution which none will try to upset, and the devouring of them is universal among all classes; for not to eat a bun was believed to cause the house of the non-eater to be burned. But then, everybody ate buns, so there was no danger of fire.

A loaf of bread baked on Good Friday was supposed to cure various ailments. A small portion of dry bread was grated into water and given to the patient, who swallowed it with large faith. There were other superstitions connected with the day which were very strange and unaccountable. One of these was the preparing of " cramp-rings," which were rings consecrated by the king and held sacred as a cure for the cramps of suffering subjects. A number of rings were placed in a silver basin, on the floor of the chapel, near a cushion, on which rested a crucifix. A piece of carpet was spread in front of the cushion, and the king knelt down, crept along on his hands and knees, in token of his humility, to the crucifix. Here, with his almoner kneeling beside him, he made his prayer, blessed the rings, and retired.

If you would have good luck, all fires must be put out on Easter Eve, and lighted afresh from flint and steel. This was a special protection against lightning strokes, as well as being an inducer of general good luck.

"On Easter Eve the fire all is quenched in every
　　place,
And fresh againe from out the flint is fetched with
　　solemn grace;
The priest doth halo this against great daungers
　　many one,
A brande whereof doth every man with greedie
　　minde take home,
That, when the fearfull storme appeares or tempest
　　black arise,
By lighting this he safe may be from stroke of
　　hurtful skies."

It was believed that, on Easter morning, the sun danced in honor of the resurrection, and hundreds of people rose before the sun to see this feat. In the *British Apollo,* printed in 1708, is this verse:

"Phœbus, the old wives say
That on Easter Day,
To the musick o' the spheres you do caper.
If the fact, sir, be true,
Pray let's the cause know,
When you have any room on your paper."

The god Phœbus replies:

"The old wives get merry
With spiced ale and sherry
On Easter, which makes them romance;
And whilst in a rout
Their brains whirl about,
They fancy *I* caper and dance."

Sir John Suckling wrote in " The Bride ":

"But oh, she dances such a way,
No sun upon an Easter Day
Is half so fine a sight."

In Scotland the sun was even more antic than in other places, for there it was expected to whirl round like a cart-wheel, and give three leaps. That the sun really did dance was solemnly discussed and argued, and combated by grave old scholars, who took the trouble to demonstrate that, while the king of day might shine more brightly on Easter morning, he did not, and could not, dance.

Another popular belief was, that one must wear for the first time, on Easter Sunday, a new article of dress, to ensure good fortune in love-affairs during the year. Can this be the origin of the Easter hat?

Here is one who must needs follow the fashion, slavishly, though he wore no Easter bonnet:

> "Last Eyster I put on my blew
>   Frock cuoat, the vust time, vier new;
> Wi' yaller buttons aal o' brass,
> That glitter'd i' the zun lik glass;
> Bekaize 'twor Eyster Zunday."

If the wind on Easter Sunday is in the east, it is best to draw *Easter water* and bathe in it to prevent ill effects from east wind, throughout the remaining months of the year.

Much importance is attached to rain falling on Easter Day, for there is an old proverb:

"A good deal of rain on Easter Day
Gives a good crop of grass, but little good hay."

If the sun shines on Easter morning it will shine till Whitsunday; and a Sussex piece of weather-lore goes so far as to say, that if the sun shines on Easter Day, it will shine, if never so little, every day during the year, while if it be a rainy Easter, there will be rain every day in the year, if only a few drops fall.

The custom of using eggs in various ways has ever been associated with Easter, and making presents of colored eggs was at one time almost universal. A writer says of this practice among the French: "With a

people so ingenious in trifles as the Parisians,
this opportunity is not lost, so that egg-
shaped articles are to be had in every con-
ceivable variety of material. One would
think that the once imperial eagle of France
had summoned all the birds of the air to
come to Paris, build their nests in shop windows, and deposit their eggs there; for go
where you will, look into whatever shop you
fancy, there you see eggs from the size of
a caraway comfit, such as is found in the
nest of a humming-bird, to one as large as
an ostrich egg. Passing along the streets
are women with barrows, crying aloud
'Des œufs! des œufs!' ('Eggs! eggs!')."

In days when old and young alike received these eggs, the demand for them was
such that they commanded great prices.
After they were colored, various inscrip-
tions and designs were traced on them; and
decorated eggs were exchanged by the sen-

timentally inclined, very much after the fashion of valentines.

If we stop to think anything about it, we may wonder why it is, that of all things eggs should be so closely identified with Easter time. Other people have thought about it, too, and have accounted for it in different ways.

The mysterious development of life in an egg has always been a wonder, and any one can see why it might be the symbol of the revival of nature and the springing forth of life, as it is used to illustrate many other things. Every one remembers the story of how Columbus astonished those who doubted his discoveries, by standing an egg on end; and we marvel yet at the wonderful roc's egg in the " Arabian Nights." The story of the goose which laid the golden egg is an old one, familiar to all, and the riddle of Humpty Dumpty has been given, if not guessed by every child. Who does not know what is meant by " counting chickens before they are hatched?" — which saying was originated only after people understood the tremendous possibilities and impossibilities contained in an egg. What boy has not had the experience of wonder and delight on finding a nest of birds' eggs? A particularly intelligent cook once said that, with the dozens of eggs she destroys, she always has a certain misgiving whenever she breaks so perfect and wonderful a thing.

The origin of Easter eggs seems to be a mixture of Christian and pagan legend.

With the early Christians an egg was an emblem of the resurrection; while the Romans thought of it in another way, as is shown by their egg games, which they celebrated at the time of our Easter, when they ran races on oval tracks and received eggs as prizes. These games were instituted in honor of Castor and Pollux, the twins who came forth from an egg deposited by the swan Leda.

Some think the Easter egg custom was borrowed from the Jews, who, at their passover, placed on the table two unleavened cakes, two pieces of lamb, some small fish, and a *hard egg,* which was the symbol of a bird called Ziz, concerning which the rabbis had a thousand fabulous tales.

We find these egg stories coming from different countries, and in a variety of forms. In ancient Persia there was a legend of two jealous brothers, who had a good deal of influence in the creation of things. One brother made an egg containing good spirits, and the other produced one full of evil demons; and they broke the two together, so that good and evil became mixed in the world. In memory of these brothers the present-day Persians, on a certain festival in March, present each other with colored eggs; and it may be from this that we get our similar Easter custom.

Another story tells us of a prince who, on Easter, presented a certain princess with a huge iron egg. She thought it a practical joke, and felt so insulted that she raised the egg high and dashed it to the floor, regardless of consequences. But, to her surprise, the force of the fall caused the egg to fly open, and on a beautiful lining of crystal lay a golden yolk. She took up the gold ball, and, opening it, found that it contained a crown of rubies; this opened also, and there lay a betrothal ring of beautiful diamonds. The name of this ingenious prince or the time in which he lived is not known, neither do we know more than this about the German princess; but the iron egg is surely a reality, for it may be seen in the Museum of Berlin.

In a parchment of the time of Edward I. is found this item: "Eighteen 'pence" (thirty-six cents) "for four hundred eggs to be used for Easter gifts." When has the price of eggs been so low? Less than two cents a dozen, and in Lent, too!

If Easter was celebrated in the days of dodos, what sport there must have been, and on what a gigantic scale! A sample of these huge eggs was found in the island of Madagascar, by a Frenchman, who, in 1850, dug up some of them which measured thirteen and a half inches in length, and eight and a half inches in diameter. The shells were as thick as an orange rind, and held eight quarts and a half, or as much as twelve dozen eggs would contain. In the days when these eggs were fresh, one could have lived very comfortably all through Lent on one egg!

Another symbol of Easter quite as familiar as the egg is the Easter hare, which, strangely enough, is very closely connected with the moon. There were all sorts of fancies with regard to the moon, from the

phases of which the time of Easter is reckoned; and among some nations the hare is a
type of the moon itself. The Hindu and
Japanese artists painted the hare across the
moon's disc, while the Chinese represent the
moon as a rabbit pounding rice in a mortar.

Here are two versions of the story which
explains the " hare in the moon." The first
is: Buddha once took upon himself the form
of a hare that he might feed a hungry fellow
creature, and was translated in that form
to the moon, where he evermore lives. But
this is a very inferior version of the story
of the starving tiger and her cubs whom
Buddha fed with his mortal body.

The second hare and moon legend says
that when Indra, disguised as a famishing
pilgrim, was praying for food, the hare, hav-.
ing nothing else to give him, threw itself
into the fire that it might be roasted for his
benefit; and the grateful Indra translated
the animal to the moon; and some star-

gazers have strained their eyes and imaginations till they think they see him there. The mythical natural history of the Hindu tells us that hares dwell on the shores of the lake of the moon.

The strands of these hare, moon, and Easter yarns have become so twisted in the heads of some unthinking people that children are sent out to look for rabbits' eggs; and they really think that the Easter hare brings the beautiful colored eggs with which they are so delighted.

In Swabia the association is so confused that the children are forbidden to make shadow pictures of rabbits on the wall, because it is considered a *sin against the moon;* and among the colored people of the South is the strange superstition of the power as a talisman of the "left hind foot of a graveyard rabbit killed in the dark of the moon."

There is an ancient belief in the county of Warwick, England, that if the young men of the town can catch a hare and bring it to the parson of the parish before ten o'clock on Easter morning, he is bound to give them a calf's head and a hundred eggs for their breakfast, and a groat in money.

In former times Easter week was celebrated with many sports, which were enjoyed by young and old. The children made gifts of colored eggs, which they rolled down-hill till they broke; the one whose egg held out longest was the luckiest one, and claimed all the eggs. We do not know whether or not it was a part of the game for the victor to share his spoils with his playmates, but it is to be hoped so.

The game of ball was a favorite sport in which the town authorities engaged with all dignity. We are told that " both ecclesiastics and laymen " used to play ball in the churches for *tansy cakes!* Tansy puddings are still favorite Easter dishes in many parts of England, and in some parishes the clerk carried round to each house a few cakes as an Easter offering. But during all Easter week there was as much playing and sporting as religious ceremony. Gregory of Nyssa draws a vivid picture of the joyous crowds, who, by their dress (a feature still preserved), their pleasures, and devout attendance at church, honored the festival. All labor ceased, all trades were suspended, the law-courts were closed, alms were given to the poor, and slaves were freed. In the reaction from Lent, people gave themselves up to the enjoyment of popular sports, dances, and entertainments. Our modern customs are mild repetitions of the old Easter festivities. At the beginning of Lent, society gives up its pleasures, and those who choose may rest from social labors. This period of quiet ends on Easter Day, when society may put on its new Easter bonnet and go to church. After that, it begins to bustle again; it may stop looking pious, and it may plunge again into the social eddy which it has churned for itself.

There are various Easter Monday customs peculiar to certain parts of England; of these, the *hare-scramble* and *bottle-kicking* of Hallaton are most interesting. At a remote period, not known to antiquaries, a piece of land was bequeathed to the rector conditionally, that he provide annually two hare pies, a quantity of ale, and two dozen penny loaves, to be scrambled for on each succeeding Easter morning, at the rising ground called Hare-pie Bank, about a quarter of a mile from the village of Hallaton. Of course, hares being out of season at this time of year, pies of mutton and veal were substituted. A benevolent rector of the last century made an effort to have the money applied to a better use; but the village wags raised the cry, and chalked on his walls and door as well as on the church: " No pie, no parson, and a job for the glazier." Other subsequent attempts alike failed, and on Easter Monday, at Hallaton, is the great carnival of the year.

The custom of " lifting " or " heaving " was a pretty general one in Northern England or Scotland. A " chair " was made with the hands, and the person who honored the seat was tossed into the air three times, and afterwards kissed. It was the privilege of the men to " lift " the women on Easter Monday, while the women returned the compliment upon Tuesday. It is said that on Easter Monday husbands beat their wives, and on Tuesday wives returned the favor and beat their husbands. Probably both parties knew their just deserts, and a satisfactory annual reckoning was not a bad idea, if they did not object to the method of mutual punishment.

There was also the custom among the men of taking off women's shoe-buckles, which were redeemed by a present. Next day the women possessed themselves of buckles from the men's shoes, which were bought back by money or presents.

But of all these rude methods of "give and take," some one writing from Warwickshire, in 1849, says that "the woman's heaving-day was the most amusing. Many a time have I passed along the streets inhabited by the lower orders of people, and seen parties of jolly matrons assembled round tables on which stood a foaming tankard of ale. There they sat in all the pride of absolute sovereignty, and woe to the luckless man that dared to invade their prerogatives! As sure as he was seen he was pursued, as soon as he was pursued he was taken, and as soon as he was taken he was 'heaved' and kissed, and compelled to pay sixpence for leave and leisure to depart."

A grave clergyman, who happened to be passing through Lancashire on Easter Tuesday, was staying an hour or two at an inn.

He was astonished by three or four lusty women, who rushed into his room, saying they had come to " lift him." The clergyman stood aghast at such an intrusion, and asked them to interpret their unknown tongue. " Why, your reverence," they explained, " we've come to lift ye 'cause its Easter Tuesday. All us women was hove yesterday, and us heaves the men to-day — and in course it's our rights and duties to heave 'em." But, after a little parley, the divine persuaded his visitors to relinquish their " rights and duties " for half a crown.

In the thirteenth century there was a custom of seizing all ecclesiastics who walked abroad, between Easter and Pentecost (because the apostles were seized by the Jews), and making them purchase their liberty with money.

Upon Thursday of Easter week it was a custom, for many years, for the English king and queen to wash the feet of as many poor subjects as they were years old. Queen Elizabeth, when thirty-nine years old, performed for the last time in her life this ceremony in memory of the similar act of Christ. King James II. was the last monarch to observe this rite. The water used was mixed with sweet herbs, and, after washing, the sign of the cross was made on the feet, and gifts were presented to the people.

Cardinal Wolsey also performed a similar office in 1530, to fifty-nine poor men, and it is stated that he gave every one of them "twelve pence in money, three ells of good canvas to make them shirts, a pair of new shoes, a cast of red herring, and three white herrings; and one of them two shillings."

As a part of the joy and freedom of Easter time, music is indispensable. Our thought of Easter is made vivid with flowers and music; and who has not been deeply moved by the wonderful chorus which closes Gounod's "Redemption." "Unfold! Unfold!

Ye portals everlasting!" will be sung as long as Easter is remembered, and its power will impress more than sermon or ritual.

The first Easter hymns were sung in the old cloisters behind gray walls amid prayers and penances; the words were austere, and the music strangely monotonous and severe. There seems little in the life of a monk to call forth much poetry or song, but he had the Old Testament, rich in symbolism and imagery from which to draw inspiration, and though the early poetry was restricted to very narrow limits, it often expressed bold realism and strong feeling. The whole nature of the mediæval monk burst forth in religious expression, every other avenue being closed to him, and his poetry, song, and prayer show the intensity of his inner life.

The earliest Easter hymn of which we have any knowledge takes us back to the fourth century. Its author is St. Ambrose,

and it was probably written about the year
340:

> "This is the very day of God, —
> Serene with holy light it came, —
> In which the stream of sacred blood
> Swept over the world's crime and shame.
>
> .   .   .   .
>
> O, admirable Mystery!
> The sins of all are laid on Thee;
> And Thou, to cleanse the world's deep stain,
> As man, doth bear the sins of men.
> What can be ever more sublime!
> That grace might meet the guilt of time.
> Love doth the bonds of fear undo,
>   And death restores our life anew!"

This hymn probably loses much of its force
through translation, but it sufficiently expresses the religious thought of the time.

There are other hymns, many of them
full of religious dogma, which impress us
with the inexorable severity of the author's
idea; others are singularly beautiful, and
express the passionate love of the monk for
Christ and the Church.

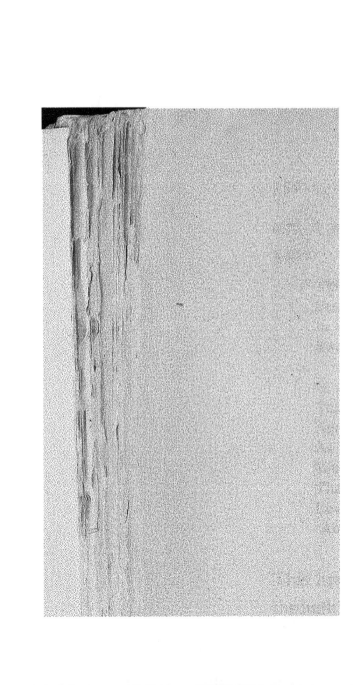

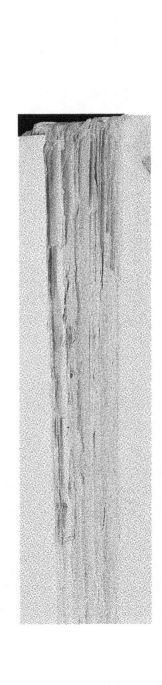

The hymns of later times are broader in thought and more elaborate in musical form, and the examples of Easter music which are now sung in the churches are among the most beautiful ever written.

Our thought of a modern Easter Sunday pictures a bright morning, birds singing, everybody in good spirits, and everybody going to church; for even those who usually must be argued or scolded into going, will adopt church ways as a matter of course on Easter Sunday. Children, especially, readily fall in with usages that combine cheerfulness with reverence, and, having once attended an Easter service, will never forget the flowers and music, however much of the sermon may have escaped them. The custom in many of our modern churches of distributing flowers to the children is a charming and touching one. Indeed, the children have come to feel that the Easter service is especially devoted to them.

The Easter lily and resurrection anthem speak a language at once personal and universal. They convey unmistakably a sentiment which appeals to the common taste and imagination; and as each Easter festival comes round, our associations of it are enriched, our religious instincts are quickened, and we have a clearer knowledge of the words with which the early Christians greeted each other on Easter morning, "Christ is risen!"

MAY DAY

MAY DAY

"Come, my Corinna, come; and coming, mark
How each field turns a street, each street a park
Made green and trimmed with trees; see how
Devotion gives each house a bough
Or branch; each porch, each door, ere this
An ark, a tabernacle is
Made up of white thorn neatly interwove;
As if here were those cooler shades of love.
  Can such delights be in the street
  And open fields, and we not see't?
  Come, we'll abroad; and let's obey
  The proclamation made for May:
And sin no more as we have done. by staying;
But, my Corinna, come, let's goe a-Maying."
                          —ROBT. HERRICK.

MAY DAY

"Is not thilke the mery moneth of May
When love lads masken in fresh aray?
How falles it, then, we no merrier beene,
Ylike as others, girt in gaudy green?"
— SPENCER.

"The flowery May who from her green lap throws
The yellow cowslip and the pale primrose,

.   .   .   .

Thus we salute thee with our early song,
And welcome thee and wish thee long."

IN these days people cannot stop amid
the sweep of twentieth-century events to
devote themselves to special rites on this
spring day; there seems to be no time for
it; and so many other things are of greater
importance, the quaint old May-day customs
are fast dying out. It is not because people
have forgotten how to play. Every one

157

knows that impulse, which comes with the first summer wind and the first rush of birds, to shake off all work and walk straight out into the country as far as he can; and no one cares to resist that delicious spring feeling which communicates exhilaration to everything. We may like to express our spring pleasures just as positively, but it is by more individual methods than did the young people of two hundred years ago.

On May-day in the country villages there may be found, now and then, a remnant of enthusiasm among the young people in the hanging of May-baskets, and a few other simple demonstrations, but of the pageants of former May-days we have only the memories which old chroniclers have handed down to us. In the ceremonies devoted to May-day were elements of the ancient sun-worship and of the Roman observances in honor of the goddess Flora, while the May-pole and its attendant displays were relics of the nature-worship of the East. To these were added various amusements popular at different times. It may be reasoned that impulses which were a result of decided changes of season would be strongest in a northern climate, where sensations, like tree-sap and young buds, were set free after a bound up winter; so in early days there was developed in England greater enthusiasm for May-day sports and festivals than was found in more southern countries.

On the first of May all manner of sports, music, and dancing were indulged in, and were supposed to be a good augury for the success of the crops for the coming season. In the "Survey of London," Stowe says that on May-day in the morning, every man would walk into the meadows and green woods to rejoice their spirits with the beauty and odor of flowers, and with the harmony of singing birds. "I find that the citizens of London, of all estates, lightly, in every parish, or sometimes two or three parishes together, had their several mayings, and did fetch May-poles with divers warlike shews, with good archers, morrice-dancers, and other devices for passtime, all the day long; and towards the evening they had stage-plaies and bone-fires in the streets."

In the reign of Henry VI. the aldermen and sheriffs of London, being on May-day at the Bishop of London's wood, and having had there " a worshipful dinner for themselves and other comers," the Monk of Bury sent them his commendation of the event in these lines:

> " Mighty Flora, goddess of fresh flow'rs
> Which clothed hath the soil in lusty greene,
> Made buds to spring with her sweet show'rs
> By influence of the sun sheene,
> To do pleasaunce of intent full ·clene
> Unto the states which now sit here
> Hath verily sent down her daughter dear."

These early May morning excursions into wood and field were enjoyed by all, old and

young. There is a description of one of
these May-walks given by one who was in
the mood to appreciate the pleasure of others,
though he was rather a melancholy spectator.
Ralph Cunnynghame, in a letter to his
cousin, writes on May-day, 1610:

" Last night I slept but ille soe was awake
in the dawne of day, and forth to coole my
brayne in the freshe dewinesse of the earlie
morne. There was a tumult of sweete
sound from the throat of a thousand birdes
till alle the ayre both far and neare, was
fulle of theire jubilate, and all the breath
of the morne was laden with the bitter fragrance of Maye " (hawthorn). " Soe I
wandered, my heart now calme within me,
with a blessed peace, till I came to that deare
spott where I first beheld my Love in all her
beautie, and there I sat me downe in deepe
meditation. How long I sat there I know
not, but I was aroused from my thoughtful-
nesse by the merrie sound of pypinge and

sweet laughter of youths and maydens, and
presentlie over the hill came a partie, the
most joyous that ever I have seen, that had
gone forth at dawne to gather the Maye,
and nowe were returninge to the village with
pyping and songe, alle laden with the blossoms lyke greate heapes of fragrant snowe.
Soe they past me and were gone, the noise
of manie voices and of musick growing
fainter till it was nigh stilled by the dis-
tance.

"They have deckt the village alle out,
lintel and beame, with those blossoms, and
alle is joyousnesse and mirth.   To-day I
went forthe with John to behold them raise
the May-pole, alle bedeckt with flowers, and
streaming ribands wreathed upon greate
hoopes hangyinge from the top of the pole.
This they raised with vast shoutings of merrie voices.   This done, sundrie youths and
maydens took eache one riband that hung
from the pole, and, with musick, danced in

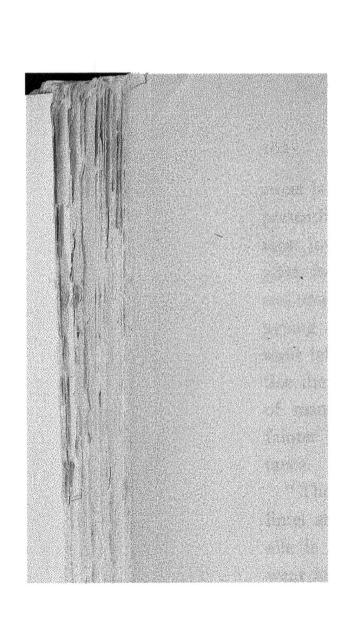

and out and back and forth but ever around
the pole, and nigher it, till with their dancing they had woven the ribands into prettie
patternes from the top to the bottom, manie
standing around watching the joyous sight.
All the morning they have been dancing
and making merrie, the Landlord of the
Bull's Heade having broached a great barrel
of October ale for their pleasuring. I tell
thee this to lett thee see howe here they celebrate the coming of Maye, though I could
enjoy it not fullie myself, being distracted
with other thoughts."

In olden times the May-feast was one
of the great events of the year, and town and
village made it a day of revelry and rejoicing. Long before sunrise on May morning
parties of young people went to the near-by
woods and fields to gather the sweet-scented
hawthorn; this became such a part of the
festivities that gathering of hawthorn came
to be spoken of as " gathering the May."

The leading feature, however, of May-
day sports was raising the May-pole which
had been brought into the town with much
ceremony, and the citizens, old and young,
devoted themselves to these pleasures with
unstinted zeal. An old English writer describes this rather showy event:

" They have twentie or fortie yoke of
Oxen, every One havyng a sweete Nosegaie
of flowers placed on the tippe of his hornes,
and these Oxen drawe home this Maie-pole,
which is covered all over with Flowers and
Herbes, bounde rounde aboute with strynges,
from the top to the bottome, and sometyme
painted with variable colours, with two or
three hundred men, women, and children
following it, with great devotion. And this
being reared up, with handkerchiefs and
flagges streamyng on the toppe, thei strawe
the grounde aboute, binde greene boughes
about it, sett up Summer Hauses, Bowers,
and Arbors hard by it. And then fall thei

to banquet and feast, to leape and daunce
aboute it."

It was customary to have a Lord of May
as well as Queen of May, but that was long
ago, as the language of their description
shows. " The May King, Robin Hood, was
to have a baldrick of blue tarantine silver
embroidered. The May Queen, Maid
Marian, was to be habited in watchet-col-
ored tissue, and her two maidens were to
have white courtpies, with a girdle of silver
bandekin; they were to have tabards, or
short jackets, with girdles of cloth of silver."

At evening, when the great bonfires were
lighted, the Queen of May, who had presided
over the festivities during the day, withdrew
with her companions, and the King of May
was left to conduct the revels of the night,
which often lasted till the next morning, and
were sometimes carried to great excess.

It is said that in his younger days King
Henry VIII. delighted to rise with the sun

on May mornings, and, with a company from his court, ride into the woods a-maying. An old writer of the time tells us, in very old English, and with a reckless disregard for orthography, of one of King Henry's May-days:

" The king and the quene accōpanyed with many lordes & ladies roade to the high grounde of shoters hil to take the open ayre, and as they passed by the way, they espied a cōpany of tall yomen, clothed all in grene whodes & bowes & arrowes, to the number of ii.C.

" Then one of them, which called him selfe Robyn hood, came to the kyng, desyring him to se his men shoote & the kyng was cōtent. Then he whisteled & al the ii.C archers shot and losed at once & then he whisteled agayne & they likewyse shot agayne, their arrowes whisteled by craft of the head, so that the noyes was straunge and great, and much pleased the kynge and quene and all the company. All these archers were of the kynges garde and had thus appareled them selves to make solace to the kyng. Then Robin hood desyred the kyng and quene to come into the green wood & to se how the outlawes live.

" The kynge demaunded of ye quene & her ladyes, if they durst adventure to go into the wood with so many outlaws. Then the quene sayde, that if it pleased him, she was content; then the hornes blewe tyl they came to the wood under shoters hil, and there was an Arber made of boowes with a hal, and a great chāber and an inner chamber, very well made, and covered with floures & swete herbes, whiche the kynge muche praysed.

" Then said Robyn hood, Sir Outlaws brekefastes is venyson, and therefore you must be content with such fare as we use. Then the kyng and quene sat downe, & were served with venyson and wyne by Robin

hood and his men, to their great contenta-
cion."

In England, in the last century, the milk-
maids' dance formed a very pretty feature
of May-day shows. There was much rivalry
in preparing the " garland," which was built
of polished milk-pails and other articles of
the dairy, silver cups, tankards, salvers, and
similar things which could be begged or
borrowed from the neighbors. These uten-
sils were arranged in the form of a pyramid,
and decorated with flowers, leaves, and gay
ribbons. The " garland " was carried from
house to house while the milkmaids danced
around, to the music of a fiddler.

In some places, instead of the tin garland,
it was the custom to lead a cow about, her
horns gilded and her body decorated with
ribbons, green leaves, and flowers.

Among the Irish and Scotch Highlanders
May-day was known as " Beltine," or, " The
day of Belens fire," and among the observ-

ances of the day are found superstitions which entered into so many of their celebrations.

In Pennant's "Tour of Scotland, 1771," is described the May-day ceremony:

"On the first day of May in the Highlands of Scotland, the herdsmen of every village hold their 'Bel-tein.' They cut a square trench on the ground, make a fire of wood, on which they dress a large caudle of eggs, butter, oatmeal, and milk, and bring, besides the ingredients of the caudle, plenty of beer and whiskey; for each of the company must contribute something.

"The rites begin with spilling some of the caudle on the ground, by way of libation; on that, every one takes a cake of oatmeal, upon which are raised square knobs, each dedicated to some particular being, the supposed preserver of their flocks and herds, or to some animal, the real destroyer of them. Each person then turns his face to

the fire, breaks off a knob, and, flinging it
over his shoulder, says: 'This I give to
thee, — preserve thou my horses; this to
thee, — preserve thou my sheep;' and so on.
After that, they use the same ceremony to
the noxious animals. When the ceremony
is over they dine on the caudle; and, after
the feast is finished, what is left is hid by
two persons deputed for that purpose; but on
the next Sunday they reassemble and finish
the reliques of the first entertainment."

There was an ancient superstition among
the natives in the village of Barvas in the
Isle of Lewis, that if a woman was the first
to cross the Barvas River on May-day, the
salmon would not come into it for a whole
year. To guard against this disastrous pos-
sibility, a man was appointed every year to
cross the river as soon as sunrise, and no
woman dared stir out till this important citi-
zen had fulfilled his annual duty.

The poet Gay describes another first of May superstition:

"Last May-day fair I searched to find a snail
  That might my secret lover's name reveal;
Upon a gooseberry bush a snail I found,
For always snails near sweetest fruit abound.
I seized the vermin; home I quickly sped,
And on the hearth the milk-white embers spread.
Slow crawled the snail, and if I right can spell,
In the soft ashes marked a curious L.
O, may this wondrous omen lucky prove,
For L is found in Luberkin and Love!"

Another superstition for the day is that if you look through smoked glass into an unused well, you will see your future husband or wife. And another: Throw a ball of yarn into an old cellar or barn, and wind, repeating the words:

"I wind, I wind, my true love to find,
  The color of his hair, the clothes he'll wear,
  The day he is married to me."

If you are patient and wind long enough (though the time isn't stated), your "true love" will appear and wind with you.

Although a few of these tricks of divination may have been tried, they were not an important feature.

May-day ceremonies were for the people, and had no purpose beyond that of pure enjoyment; and it is interesting to know how even the town officials entered into the amusements. We know the cost of some of the old-time May-poles, for the price may be found in the church·wardens' accounts. Parishes of London vied with each other in the height and decoration of their May-poles. One at Basing Lane was forty feet high, and one was erected in the Strand a hundred and thirty feet high. So high and big was it, that some of the sailors of the Lord High Admiral worked four hours to raise it up with ropes and pulleys. Then there was the May-pole which was kept in Shaft Alley, resting on hooks above the doors of the houses; but after the sermon preached at Paul's Cross Church, in which this May-pole was denounced as a symbol of idolatry, it was sawn up and burned, each man taking the piece that his house measured.

We can easily see why, in America, these festivals have declined, or, more truly, were never established; for the Puritans were great enemies of May-games and the May-pole, and, during Cromwell's time, all May-sports were prohibited, and May-poles ordered to be taken down and burned.

By the time Charles II. was made king, the people were thoroughly tired of the eleven years of Puritan rule, and when their May-day celebrations were allowed again, summer was sung and danced in more joyously and riotously than ever, and the roisterers trimmed the houses of prominent Puritans with not very pleasant decorations.

This enmity of the Puritans was partly political and partly religious. They objected because May-games were commanded by the

" Book of Sports," both of James I. and Charles I., and also because they had been allowed in Catholic times, and so were denounced as idolatrous.

One Puritan preacher said: " If Moses was angry when he saw the people dance around a golden calf, well may we be angry to see people dancing about a post; " and another said: " The rude rabble set up their Ensign of Idolatry and Profaneness even in Cheapside."

A rhyme of 1646 reads:

" And harmless May Poles are rail'd upon
    As if they were the towers of Babylon."

In a pamphlet of 1691, reference was made to these Puritan " brethren " when it said: " Remember the blessed times when everything in the world that was displeasing and offensive to the brethren went under the name of horrid and abominable Popish superstitions; organs and May-poles, surplices and long hair; cathedrals and playhouses; set forms of prayer and painted glass; fonts and apostles' spoons, — a long list."

No wonder, then, that the first May-day celebration in New England, with its May-pole and reckless jollity, was denounced by the Pilgrim fathers, who felt the responsibility of keeping the new American continent free from sin.

The May-pole of Merrymount was set up in 1627, when lawless Thomas Morton and his motley crew landed on the shores of Boston Bay, and with loud revels celebrated the first of May.

The Pilgrims had been settled at Plymouth, twenty miles farther south, for six years. Scattered along the seven hundred miles of seacoast there were but two hundred and fifty people, most of them at Plymouth, and in this wilderness it seems an incongruous thing that such festivities should have taken place, when the revellers might soon suffer the perils of hunger, and whose only neighbors were savages, or the devout, severe Puritans, whose influence tended to anything but lightheartedness.

But Morton and his followers possessed high spirits sufficient unto themselves, and as they had taken things into their own hands at the settlement of Quincy, it pleased them to celebrate May-day of 1627 with all the ceremonies which had been used in the most jovial English days, with many more added.

They did not carouse soberly, for, from the account of Morton himself, we know that there was a barrel of strong beer, besides a liberal supply of bottles of stronger drinks, which had been supplied for the cheer of all comers.

The May-pole itself was a pine-tree eighty feet long, wreathed with flowers and made gay with ribbons, and at the top were nailed the spreading horns of a buck.

When the holiday came, the pole was

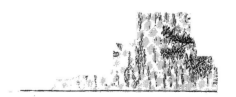

dragged to the top of Merrymount, amid the rattle of drums and the firing of flintlocks, and there set, the Indians helping with the rest. A poem suited to the occasion, written by Morton, was tacked to the pole. The author says of it: " Enigmatically composed, it pusselled the Separatists most pittifully to expound it; " and it is said that none since that day has been able to make out the sense of it, there being so little in it. Governor Bradford was impressed with its meaning enough to say: " These rimes affixed to this idoll May-pole tended to ye detraction & scandall of some persons; " but he does not go so far as to specify either the nature of the scandal or the names of the persons. But to most people the whole effusion, with the exception of the last two lines, in which the first of May is declared a holiday, is a very wordy puzzle; and Governor Bradford need not have been anxious about its evil effects. He might have been more concerned about the conduct of the company, which was far from Puritanical. While the people danced and circled around the May-pole, some one kept filling the cups, and, as he did so, sang one of Morton's songs:

> "Make greene garlons, bring bottles out;
> And fill sweet Nectar freely about,
> Uncover thy head, and feare no harme,
> For her's good liquor to keepe it warme.

> "Give to the Mellancolly man
> A cup or two of't now and than;
> This physick will soone revive his bloud,
> And make him be of a merrier mood."

Governor Bradford thought that this song also tended to unseemly merriment and excess, but his displeasure had no effect, for his authority could not be enforced beyond his settlement at Plymouth. There we have record of but one attempt to establish old English festivities in New England, when some newcomers refused to work upon Christmas Day because of their *conscientious* scruples. "So yᵉ Govʳ tould them that. if they made it a matter of conscience, he would spare them till they were better informed. So he led away yᵉ rest and left them; but when they came home at noone from their work, he found them in yᵉ streete at play, openly; some pitching yᵉ barr & some at stoole-ball, and such like sports. So he went to them, and tooke away their implements, and toulde them that it was against his conscience that they should play and others work. If they made yᵉ keeping of it a matter of devotion, let them kepe their houses, but ther should be no gameing or revelling in yᵉ streets."

We do not wonder, then, that the reports of Morton's May-festival filled the Plymouth people with horror, and that they could find nothing so heathenish to compare with it since pagan times. So Governor Bradford writes again:

"They allso sit up a May-pole, drinking

and dancing aboute it many days togeather; dancing· and frisking togither with the Indean women, as if they had anew revived & celebrated the feasts of ye Roman Goddes Flora, or ye beasly practices of ye madd Bacchanalian."

When dare-devil Morton met with such opposition, fainter-hearted ones had no courage for pleasuring in the face of those awesome Pilgrim fathers, so we may say that the delights of the old May-day festival never came to this side of Merrie England.

All over Europe the songs of spring and May-time are to be found, some of the melodies being very beautiful. The music of May-day endured long after the ceremonies ceased to be, the words of the songs outliving some of the tunes. Here is an old Lancashire carol:

> "Come, lads, with your bills,
> To the work we'll away.
> We'll gather the boughs
> And we'll celebrate May.

"We'll bring our loads home
As we've oft done before,
And leave a green bough .
At each pretty maid's door."

This is a May-eve song, a work of some
crude composer:

"If we should wake you from your sleep,
Good people listen now,
Our yearly festival we keep,
And bring a Maythorn bough;
An emblem of the world it grows,
The flowers its pleasures are,
And many a thorn bespeaks its woes,
Its sorrow and its care."

Here is a stanza of an old carol:

"The rose is red, the rose is white,
The rose is in my garden;
I would not part with my sweetheart
For twopence-halfpenny farden."

It would not be a very great calamity if
even these old May-songs should be forgotten with the old May-day ceremonies,
for every year the spirit of May comes, and

with it new songs from the throat of every bird and the heart of every man. Cromwell could, with his " Barebone's Parliament," prohibit May-poles and May-sports in London, and the devout Plymouth Pilgrims could frown down open demonstrations of May-day pleasures, but neither Cromwell nor the Pilgrim fathers can prevent the unconscious nature-worship which springs up in every heart, and which will find expression in spite of parliaments and creeds.

We may not care for a May-pole the size of a ship's mast, nor for the old-time decked-out May-queen who sat on a throne of roses and held a sceptre of rushes, but there is not one who does not, on every sweet May morning, sing in spirit the closing lines of the old poem:

"While time serves and we are but decaying,
  Come, my Corinna, come, let's goe a-Maying."

HALLOWE'EN

HALLOWE'EN

"There is a world in which we dwell,
And yet a world invisible!
- And do not think that naught can be,
Save only what with eyes ye see;
I tell ye, that, this very hour,
Had but your sight a spirit's power,
Ye would be looking, eye to eye,
At a terrific company!"

. . . .

"I tell ye the story this chill Hallowe'en,
For it suiteth the Spirit eve;
The spirits are pulling the sere dry leaves
Of the shadowy forest down.
And howl the gaunt reapers that gather the sheaves,
With the moon, o'er their revels, to frown.
To-morrow ye'll find all the spoils in your path,
And ye'll speak of the wind and the sky;
But oh, could ye see them to-night, in their wrath,
I ween ye'd be frenzied of eye!"

HALLOWE'EN

"In the hinder end of harvest upon All Hallow Eve,
Quhen our gude nichbours rydis (now gif I reid
  . richt)
Some bucklet on a benwood and some on a bene,
Ay trottand into troupes fra the twilicht."
                                    —KING JAMES VI.

How many times have those people,
vaguely called Ancient Heathen, been re-
sponsible for inaugurating habits which have
been blindly followed by all nations for
thousands of years. It may be that these
ancients were particularly original and far-
sighted, and, having satisfied all the demands
of their own lives, prophetically discerned
the needs of future people, and established
customs which would adapt themselves to all
races for all times.

But it is easier to suppose that certain traits inherent in human nature have been, and always will be, expressed, regardless of example. If the first man was a superstitious one, then the last man will have at least some little superstition hanging about him.

People have been credulous in supernatural things from the beginning of time, and the origin of certain traditions, like the absolute origin of superstition, can never be reached. Many customs which prevail have been preserved simply as a matter of thoughtless habit, others by the power of imagination, which has made vague beliefs appear as realities, and which has kept alive certain observances, when all knowledge of their causes has long been forgotten.

The origin of traditions connected with Hallowe'en, like those surrounding many other subjects, is lost in antiquity; and though the traditions themselves are composed of such material as the fancies of people, they seem to have survived shocks which would destroy a more substantial thing.

Even in these practical, matter-of-fact times, we meet people who have their superstitions about dreams, folk-medicine, weather-proverbs, the number thirteen, and the fulfilment of wishes upon various conditions; and every one is familiar with the witch, wizard, hobgoblin, and evil eye of past days.

Our forefathers looked upon nature with reverence and horror, and delighted to astonish themselves with the apprehensions of witchcraft, prodigies, charms, and enchantments. There was not a village in England that had not at least one ghost in it; the churchyards were all haunted, every village green had its circle of fairies, and there was scarce a shepherd to be met with who had not seen a spirit.

At times superstitions have been exaggerated into insane foreboding. Nature's simplest phenomena meant some disaster; dreams and visions of the morbid were accepted as divine inspirations; the commonest object was raised to the importance of an oracle; demon-music was heard in the wind, and destiny read in the stars.

There were always some, however, who, during the times of greatest excitement, kept their senses, and, by coolly directing suspicion to one who might be a witch or have an evil eye, could often rid themselves of many a disagreeable person; so the practical man made especial use of the superstitions of his neighbors.

Talk about supernatural things was almost as universal and interesting as talk about the weather. Gay, the poet, tells us about —

"Those tales of vulgar sprites
Which frightened boys relate on winter nights,
How cleanly milkmaids meet the fairy train,
How headless horses drag the clinking chain,

Night roaming ghosts by saucer eyeballs known,
The common spectres of each country town."

Many ancient popular divinations were associated with a particular season, and the observations connected with Hallowe'en probably represent a heathen festival whose celebration consisted in giving to the departed, at harvest-time, his share of the fruits of the earth. At this time the spirits of the dead were supposed to walk abroad, and all practices, as are shown by ancient magic and savage custom, were of such a nature as would be favorable for spirits to manifest themselves.

In these ceremonies, water, fire, all the elements of nature, with the sun, moon, and stars, were resorted to, that the spirits might easily find expression; but there seems to have been little success in gaining very much general knowledge, for in modern times only those superstitions have the greatest interest for us which are based on the broadest and

most human foundation — those connected
with death and marriage.

So the custom of prying after knowledge
about future partners for life, is but a sur-
vival of an older practice, and though the
special intention of many ceremonies has
been forgotten, Hallowe'en customs show
the lively desire of all young people to look
into the future with reference to marriage.

However it came about, it is quite certain that the evening of the thirty-first of
October has been stamped with a peculiar
character, by the popular imagination. The
notion prevails that the supernatural rules.
Spirits walk the earth, shades haunt all
convenient places, spooks hide in every cor-
ner, and hobgoblins run wild.

In spite of all this uncanniness, instead
of being paralyzed with fear, people court
these unseen things, who have the reputa-
tion of being friendly devils, and who will
give valuable information upon important

subjects if approached rightly, and if one complies with some simple condition.

The questions with which these invisibles are taxed usually refer to somebody's love-affair; that being settled, all minor matters will easily adjust themselves.

If these spirits take such interest in mortals that they are willing to show gratuitously how young people may solve their hearts' riddles, surely one cannot hesitate to perform a few simple rites.

First there is the oracle of the nuts. A number of nuts are named for lovers and put upon a bed of coals. If a nut jumps, the lover will prove unfaithful, — probably he is a man of spirit, and finds conditions too hot for him. If a nut blazes and burns, he surely loves the girl who named the nut, — the fires of love rage in his bosom. If both nuts named for a maid and her lover burn together, they will be married. It is well that anxious ones performing this ceremony be provided with very dry, combustible nuts and a fine bed of red coals. An early eighteenth-century poet has taken this ceremony so seriously that he has put it into verse:

"These glowing nuts are emblems true
    Of what in human life we view;
    The ill-matched couple fret and fume,
    And thus in strife themselves consume;
    Or from each other wildly start
    And with a noise forever part.
    But see this very happy pair,
    Of genuine love and truth sincere,
    With mutual fondness, while they burn
    Still to each other kindly turn,
    And as the vital sparks decay
    Together gently sink away
    Till life's fierce ordeal being past
    Their mingled ashes rest at last."

Nuts seem to have been used very early for purposes of divination. The Roman boys made some use of nuts in their sports, for Horace speaks of it; and in marriage ceremonies among the Romans, the bridegroom threw nuts about the room for the boys to scramble for. In the ancient Romish calendar nuts are referred to, as some religious use was made of them.

Gay, in the " Spell," refers to the nut-burning ceremony:

> " Two hazel nuts I threw into the flame,
>   And to each nut I gave a sweetheart's name;
>   This, with the loudest bounce me sore amaz'd,
>   That, in a flame of brightest color blaz'd;
>   As blaz'd the nut, so may thy passion-grow,
>   For thus the hazel nut did brightly glow!"

Doctor Goldsmith, in the " Vicar of Wakefield," says that " the rustics religiously cracked nuts on All Hallow's Eve," and nuts are so much used in England and Scotland that Hallowe'en is called " Nut-crack night."

Burns gives a picture of the nut-burning rite:

> " The auld guidwife's weel hoordet nits,
>   Are round and round divided,

And monie lads' and lassies' fates,
  Are there that night decided;
Some kindle, couthie, side by side,
  An' burn togither trimly;
Some start awa' wi' saucy pride,
  And jump out owre the chimlie
      Fu high that night."

An old Scotch method of seeing future things, is to pull a cabbage, blindfolded.

A young woman would grope her way to the cabbage-patch and pull the first plant she stumbled against. The amount of earth clinging to its root showed the amount of her dowry, the shape and size indicated the appearance and height of the future husband, while the flavor of the heart and stem signified his disposition.

In the old Scottish Hallowe'en game each took home the stalk and laid it behind the outer door, and the first person to enter next morning was to be the future husband.

This old gruesome rhyme is supposed to refer to this cabbage pulling:

"One, two, three, four, five, six, seven.
If all are white, all go to heaven;
If one is black as Mustaph's evil,
He'll soon be screechin' wi' the devil."

Another Scotch rhymester has described the ceremony of the kail stalk:

"Then first and foremost through the kail,
Their slocks maun a' be sought ance:
They steek their e'en, an grip an wale
For muckle anes, and straight anes."

An appropriate Hallowe'en method of inducing visions directs a young lady to eat an apple while standing before a mirror combing her hair. The future husband will look into the glass over her shoulder. To be effectual this must be done at midnight, but such is the unaccountable nature of woman that the test is often abandoned when the very moment of fulfilment is near at hand. After all, she would rather believe that there is a some one, somewhere, whom her thought may vaguely idealize,

than to know definitely the face and form
of one, who, after all, might disappoint
her. How much better, then, she thinks,
to spend the night in refreshing sleep, than
to try to explore the future by such uncanny
tricks, when her excited imagination is as
likely to produce a fiend as a god — or a
husband.

Another night spell is, to walk backward
several rods, out-of-doors, in the moonlight,
with a mirror, or if this is done indoors,
with a candle in one hand and a mirror in
the other, repeating the following rhyme.
A face will (without doubt!) be seen in the
glass.

"Round and round, O stars so fair!
Ye travel and search out everywhere;
I pray you, sweet stars, now show to me
This night who my future husband shall be."

Many of the rhymes are written to be
said by girls, it being taken for granted that
only they are curious about matrimonial

affairs. Should there, however, be inquisitive young men, this Scotch test is good for those who have plenty of courage and a good constitution. "You go out, one or more, for this is a social spell, to a south-running spring or rivulet, where three lairds' lands meet, and dip your left shirt-sleeve. Go to bed in sight of a fire, and hang your wet sleeve before it to dry. Lie awake, and sometime near midnight an apparition, having the exact figure of the grand object in question, will come and turn the sleeve as if to dry the other side of it."

It is not stated whether you detach the sleeve from your shirt for these processes, nor is the recipe given for curing your next morning's feelings, which have naturally resulted from a wetting, a sleepless night, and, very probably, a failure to see the *grand object* you expected at midnight.

Burns tells us of the Widow Leezie, who,

perhaps, having exhausted all others, was hard put for a new test, and used this one, originally intended for mankind alone:

> "A wanton widow Leezie was,
>   As cantie as a kitlin;
> But och! that night among the shaws
> · She got a fearfu' settlin'!
> She thro' the whins, an' by the cairn,
>   An' owre the hill gaed scrievin;
> Where three lairds' lan's met at the burn,
>   To dip her left sark-sleeve in,
>   Was bent that night."

Another trick was to go out at night alone, into the barn, and take the implement for winnowing corn, called in Scotland a " wecht," go through the motions of winnowing three times, and the future husband will pass through the barn, so —

> "Meg fain wad to the barn gaen,
>   To winn three wechts o' naething;
> But for to meet the deil her lane,
>   She pat but little faith in:
> She gies the herd a pickle nits,
>   An' twa red cheekit apples,

> To watch, while for the barn she sets,
> In hopes to see Tam Kipples
>   That vera night."

Gay, in his "Pastorals," describes a Hallowe'en custom which was sure of results, but needed much patience.

A young girl says:

> "At eve last Hallowe'en no sleep I sought,
> But to the field, a bag of hemp seed brought,
> I scattered round the seed on ev'ry side,
> And three times in a trembling accent cry'd:
> 'This hemp seed with my virgin hand I sow,
> Who shall my true love be, the crop shall mow.'"

In another verse is described the experience of a rustic maiden whose method of divination was quite easy and successful:

> "As peascods once I plucked I chanced to see
> One that was closely filled with three times three,
> Which when I crop'd, I safely home convey'd,
> And o'er the door the spell in secret laid; —
> The latch moved up, when who should first come in,
> But in his proper person — Lubberkin!"

This girl is bound to see Lubberkin in all her experiments, and she is not satisfied till she has tested all probabilities:

"I pare this pippin round and round again,
　My shepherd's name to flourish on the plain,
　I fling th' unbroken paring o'er my head,
　Upon the grass a perfect L is read."

She tries again:

"This pippin shall another tryal make,
　See from the core two kernels brown I take;
　This on my cheek for Lubberkin is worn,
　And Booby Clod on t'other side is borne;
　But Booby Clod soon drops upon the ground,
　A certain token that his love's unsound.
　While Lubberkin sticks firmly to the last;
　Oh, were his lips to mine but join'd so fast."

There are many other ways with which simple people in earnest, and wise people in sport, try to discern future things.

An easy way is for each person to melt some lead and pour it through a wedding-ring into a dish of water. The lead will cool in various shapes which may (or may not) be suggestive of future events. An ingenious imagination will see weddings in bell-shaped drops, fame in a lead torch, wealth in a horn of plenty, and travel in a trunk. In fact, one can make almost anything out of the lead shapes, and interpret them in almost any way.

There are other ways of finding out in a very few minutes what will take years to discover by more scientific methods.

Cut the letters of the alphabet from a newspaper and sprinkle them on the surface of water; the floating letters will combine to spell the name of future husband or wife.

String a raisin in the middle of a thread a yard long and let two persons take each an end of the string in his mouth; whoever, by chewing the string, reaches the raisin first, has the raisin, and (if he lives) will be the first to be wedded.

Tie a wedding-ring to a silk thread and

hold it suspended within a goblet; then repeat the alphabet slowly; whenever the ring strikes the side of the goblet, begin the alphabet again, and in this way spell out the name of your life-partner.

If a maiden wants to tempt the future, let her walk down-stairs backward, holding a lighted candle over her head. Upon reaching the bottom, if she turns around suddenly, before her will stand the wished-for one — at least, he will be there if he has any idea of what is going on; therefore he must have a previous hint, if this test is to be successful.

The crowning Hallowe'en test is made by a girl who must go directly to her room without speaking to any one, and, kneeling beside her bed, must twine together the stems of two roses (roses in October!), and repeat the following lines, looking meanwhile upon the lover's rose:

> "Twine, twine and intertwine,
> Let my love be wholly mine;

> If his heart be kind and true,
> Deeper grow his rose's hue."

If her admirer be faithful, the color of the rose will appear darker. If unfaithful, deponent saith not what happens.

In an old book of charms published in Edinburgh in 1690, entitled " Old Father Time's Bundle of Faggots Newly Bound Up," we are told that an infallible means of getting a sight of the future lady is to place on a table a glass of water in which a small piece of wood is floating. In the night you will dream of falling from a bridge into a river, and of being rescued by one whom you will see as distinctly as though you were awake. Gay says of this:

> " Last Hallowe'en I looked my love to see
> And tried a spell to call her up to me.
> With wood and water standing by my side,
> I dreamed a dream and saw my own sweet bride."

Another method is to go at midnight to a walnut-tree, walk three times around it, look up into the branches, and ask your true love to bring you some nuts.

" Last Hallow Eve I sought a walnut-tree
In hopes my true Love's face that I might see.
Three times I called, three times I walked apace;
Then in the tree I saw my true Love's face."

A very old Hallowe'en divination, which was formerly much practised by the English rustics, will tell you from what quarter of the compass the future husband or wife will come. Go out — of course, at midnight — pluck out a lock of hair and cast it to the breeze. In whatever direction it is blown, from that point will come the long-expected person. Gay, in the " Pastorals," has put all these things in verse, and refers to this one:

" I pluck this lock of hair from off my head
To tell whence comes the one that I shall wed.
Fly, silken hair, fly all the world around,
Until you reach the spot where my true love
    is found."

Another very similar way is also described in verse:

"This Lady Fly I take from off the grass,
Whose spotted back might scarlet red surpass.
Fly, Lady Bird, North, South, or East or West,
Fly where the man is found that I love best."

With such a variety of experiments suited to all sorts and conditions, and which may be practised at all times of day or night, there need not be any one who is at all doubtful as to his future in matrimonial affairs. If one spell does not satisfy, try another, try *all,* but let us be sure to settle the matter somehow, for until that is done, I fear some of us will never rest.

In Ireland upon Hallowe'en the whole family partake of the mysterious spirit of the time. Aged grandsires delight to recall their youthful days, when people expected the marvellous, and the most unaccountable things caused no wonder. Then midnight goblins lurked everywhere, women dressed in white glided about, gaunt warriors galloped through dark glens in black armor, with plumes of waving fire, and crowds of transparent figures revelled among old ruins or danced in the moonlight.

A traveller, who could not avoid making a journey on that night, played boisterous tunes on his pipe or roared a lively song to frighten away elves and hobgoblins who haunted the dark and played tricks upon quiet travellers.

While at these home gatherings the grandfathers tell stories of the good old days, the mothers sit knitting. Their past is not so far behind as to be surrounded with a pleasant mist, while enough of the future is guessed to leave no room for curiosity. But the girls are still prying. They are dumbly kneading cake with their left thumbs —a single word would break the spell, and

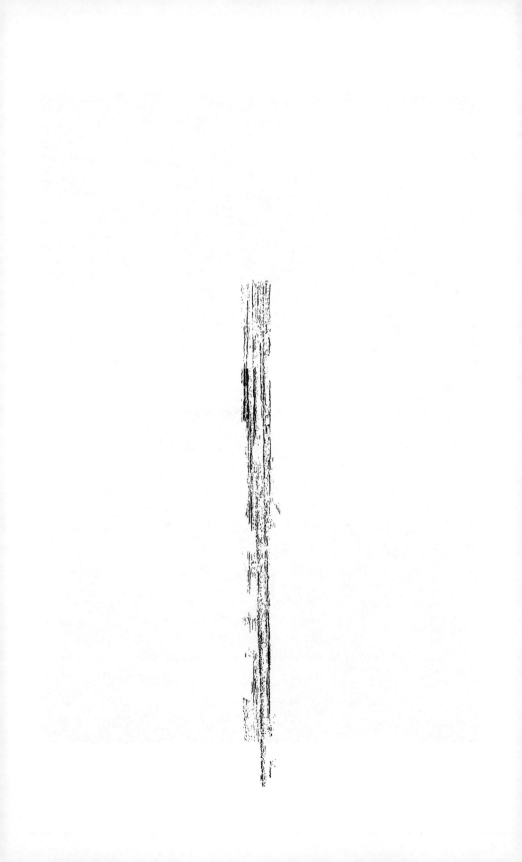

destroy the hope of seeing their future husbands in dreams, after having eaten the
mystic " dumb-cake."

While the girls are busy getting wisdom
from dumb-cakes, the boys of the family,
who care neither for past or future, indulge
in the present joys of " snap-apple." From
the ceiling is hung a skewer with an apple
stuck upon one end, and on the other a
lighted candle. Whoever is dexterous
enough to catch the apple in his mouth
takes it as a prize, while the boy who catches
the candle gets only burns. A singed head
and a mouthful of tallow is awarded to all.
To these boys Hallowe'en means only a time
to enjoy boisterous games, with plenty of
nuts and apples to play with and to eat; the
mysterious influence caught and utilized by
their elders passes entirely over their young
heads.

The Hallowe'en party described by Burns

shows how the Scotch liked to spend the
night.   The whole list of ceremonies was
gone through, with more or less success;
every lass was in high spirits, and every lad
determined that each vision should material-
ize.

The poem " Hallowe'en " opens and closes
with a picture — the various Hallowe'en
ceremonies being described in intervening
stanzas:

"Among the bonie winding banks
    Where Doon rins wimplin clear;
Where Bruce ance rul'd the martial ranks,
    An' shook his Carrick spear:
Some merry, friendly, contra-folks
    Together did convene
To burn their nits, an' pou their stocks,
    An' haud their Hallowe'en
            Fu blythe that night.

        .   .   .   .

"Wi' merry songs an' friendly cracks,
    I wat they did na weary;
And unco tales, an' funnie jokes —
    Their sports were cheap an' cheery;

Till buttered sowens, wi' fragrant lunt,
  Set a' their gabs a-steerin';
Syne, wi' a social glass o' strunt
  They parted aff careerin'
            Fu blythe that night."

THANKSGIVING

THANKSGIVING

"Lord, thou hast given me a cell,
        Wherein to dwell;
A little house, whose humble roof
        Is weather proof;
Under the spars of which I lie
        Both soft and dry;
Where thou, my chamber for to ward,
        Hast set a guard
Of harmless thoughts, to watch and keep
        Me, while I sleep.
Low is my porch as is my fate;
        Both void of state;
And yet the threshold of my door
        Is worn by th' poor,
Who thither come, and freely get
        Good words or meat.

   .   .   .   .

Some brittle sticks of thorn or briar
        Make me a fire,
Close by whose loving coal I sit,
        And glow like it.
Lord, I confess too, when I dine
        The pulse is thine,

'Tis thou that crown'st my glittering hearth
    With guiltless mirth,
And giv'st me wassail-bowls to drink
    · Spiced to the brink.
Lord, 'tis Thy plenty dropping hand
    That soils my land,
And giv'st me for my bushel sown,
    Twice ten for one.

  .   .   .   .

All these, and better, Thou dost send
    Me, to this end, —
That I should render, for my part,
    A thankful heart."
— ROB'T HERRICK.

With guiltless mirth,
And give me wassail-bowls to
Spiced to the brink.
Lord, 'tis Thy plenty dropping hand
land,
my bushel sows,
Twice ten for one.

All these, and better, Thou dost hand
Me, to this end,—
render, my part,
A thankful heart."

Thanksgiving Day

HOME FOR THANKSGIVING

THANKSGIVING

"Some hae meat that canna eat,
Some hae na' meat, but want it,
But we hae meat, and we can eat,
And sae the Lord be thankit."

— BURNS.

THANKSGIVING DAY, as annually remembered in the United States, is peculiarly an American institution; but days of thanksgiving in recognition of special mercies have been common to all Christian nations for centuries; yet, since the annual celebration of the Feast of Ingathering by the Jews, no other nation has regularly set apart one day in each year for a thanksgiving festival.

We cannot claim any originality for this institution, for the ancient Hebrews kept their feast of thanksgiving with great re-

215

joicing and religious ceremonies. This was established by Yaweh himself under directions given to Moses in Deuteronomy, the sixteenth chapter: "Thou shalt observe the feast of tabernacles, seven days after that thou hast gathered in thy corn and thy wine." They were further commanded to "rejoice in thy feast, thou, and thy son, and thy daughter," with the familiar list of man-servant, maid-servant, and Levite, stranger and fatherless, widow and orphan. The ox and ass are not included, but they doubtless had their share of the corn if not of the wine.

In Leviticus we are told that the Lord spake unto Moses, and said: "Speak unto the children of Israel, saying, The fifteenth day of the seventh month shall be the feast of tabernacles for seven days unto the Lord. . . . Ye shall do no servile work therein: also on this fifteenth day of the seventh month, when ye have gathered in the fruit of the land, ye shall keep a feast unto the Lord, seven days . . . and ye shall rejoice before the Lord your God seven days." Again, in Exodus, is mentioned " the feast of the harvest, the first fruits of thy labors, which thou hast sown in the field, and the feast of ingathering which is the end of the year, when thou hast gathered in thy labors out of the field."

All of these feasts occurred after harvest-time, when material blessings were both abundant and obvious; and the people not only had the disposition but the time to be thankful, after the labor of crop-gathering was over.

In these thanksgiving proclamations the people were commanded to take holiday, to feast and to rejoice; and all the proclamations since that day, down to those annually issued by our governors, have not improved upon this.

So great were the festivities on these

occasions of Jewish feasts that Plutarch
wrote of them: " The Jews celebrate two
feasts unto Bacchus. In the midst of the
vintage they spread tables, spread with all
manner of fruits, and live in tabernacles
made especially of palm and ivy wreaths
together. . . . A few days later they kept
another festival, which openly shows it was
dedicated to Bacchus, for they carried
boughs of palms in their hands, with which
they went into the temple, the Levites going
before, with instruments of music."

The ancient Greeks also held a feast closely
resembling that of the Jews. This feast,
which continued nine days, was called the
Feast of Demeter, in honor of Demeter, the
goddess of the corn-field and harvests. The
sacrifices offered were mostly fruits of the
soil, with oblations of wine, honey, and milk.

The Romans observed a harvest-festival
which they called Cerelia, which was as
ancient as the reign of Romulus. Proces-

sions of men and women, with music and song, went into the fields to engage in worship, rustic sports, and pleasures.

The old English Harvest Home was a festival held at time of harvest, and was celebrated with many rude and boisterous proceedings; and in the time of Egbert and Alfred, the Saxon churls kept the harvest-feasts, and the practices of the Kentish farmers in Queen Elizabeth's time were not much different. The day was spent in dancing on the village green, with rural sports, while at night great blazing bonfires were built, and great quantities of home-brewed ale were drank.

Queen Elizabeth issued a proclamation for a day of thanksgiving, saying: "On Thanksgiving Day no servile labor may be performed, and thanks should be offered for the increase and abundance of His fruits upon the face of the earth."

There was a day of national thanksgiving

in England on the defeat of the Spanish armada, and Oliver Cromwell gave directions for a day of thanks during his reign. On the discovery of the " gunpowder plot " people gave thanks, and the day was observed for more than a century. " Guy Fawkes Day " is still remembered in England and the colonies.

When George III. came to himself after his temporary fit of insanity, the whole kingdom celebrated the event, and a thanksgiving service was held in St. Paul's Cathedral.

Thanksgiving days have been held, occasionally, in Germany, France, and other nations, but we do not know of their becoming troublesome except in England. There the spirit of giving thanks was so lively that, as we have seen, any special victory in war, the recovery of a ruler from illness, the miscarriage of a plot against the government, and many other events were made an excuse for a holiday that was not found in the saints' calendar. At harvest-time, especially, the feast-days and saints' days were so numerous that the idlers neglected the very crops for which they were so anxious to be thankful, " in not taking th' oportunitie of good and serene weather offered upon the same, in time of harvest." Edward VI., seeing the necessity of work in spite of play-days, decreed that it should be " lawful to every husbandman to labor on those holy days that came in time of harvest."

Indeed, the Church and civil thanksgiving days had increased to such an extent that there were very few left for working days. Except in harvest-time in Edward's reign, no one was allowed to work on such days, and those who did were fined.

There was formerly a long religious service in the morning, a fast till four o'clock, then a public feast. Later, the church service was shortened or omitted altogether,

and the day was given up to excessive games
and sports. Not only were the harvest
thanksgiving days of importance, but the
Sabbath, saints' days, fast and feast days,
were equally times of recreation; and we
read that Latimer, who went on a holy day
to a certain church to preach, found the village deserted, the church locked, and the
people all gone a-maying!

Naturally, the English Puritans looked
with disapproval on all such degenerating
customs. In fact, these, with other offensive
practices, became so intolerable to the Puritan mind that those who had not supplied
material for the block, or Queen Mary's bonfires, decided to quit the country altogether.
This did not dampen English fervor very
much, for during the Commonwealth under
Cromwell, there were observed, in one year,
more than a hundred feast-days.

Fasts and thanksgivings (which usually
meant feasts) were the order of the day,

and supplemented each other perfectly, for after days spent in fasting and church service, people were allowed "a convenient time for their repast and refreshing;" but at the same time they were advised to "beware of all excess and riot, tending to gluttony and drunkenness." This quotation from "Mandeville Travels" gives the whole programme of one of these typical holidays:

"The Comoners upon festyfulle dayes, when thei scholden gon to Chirche to serve God, then gon thei to Tavernes."

The Pilgrims who went to Holland in such disgust of English ways became somewhat mollified, and grew accustomed to Dutch fast and feast days, which were celebrated in a way more fitted to the occasion, as the poor were allowed to feast with their more favored neighbors.

That the Puritans clung to the intense religious idea which they connected with

thanksgiving days, is shown by the manner
in which they celebrated these occasions
when uninfluenced by the customs of a surrounding nation. The first thanksgiving
service held in North America was observed
with religious ceremonies conducted by an
English minister, in the year 1578, on the
shores of Newfoundland. This clergyman
accompanied the expedition under Frobisher,
who settled the first English colony in America. The records of this day have been
preserved in part, in the rules and regula-
tions which were carried out during the
expedition:

"In primus: — To banish swearing, dice
and card playing, and filthy communication,
and to serve God twice a day, with the ordinary services of the Church of England.
On Monday morning, May twenty-seventh,
1578, aboard the *Ayde,* we received all, the
communion by the minister of Gravesend,
prepared as good Christians toward God,

and resolute men for all fortunes; and toward night we departed toward Tilbury Hope. Here we highly prayed God, and altogether, upon our knees, gave him due humble and hearty thanks, and Maister Wolfall, a learned man appointed by her Majesty's council to be our minister, made unto us a goodlye sermon, exhorting all especially to be thankful to God for His strange and marvelous deliverance in those dangerous places."

Another similar service was held by the Popham colony, who settled at Sagadahoc on the Maine coast, in 1607. The record says: " Sundaye being the nineth of August, in the morninge, the most part of our hole company of both our ships, landed on this island, where the cross standeth, and thear we heard a sermon delyvred unto us by our preacher, giving God thanks for our happy meetinge and safe aryvall into this country; and so returned aboard again."

The Thanksgiving of the Pilgrims at Plymouth is more familiar. After the experiences of their first year in America they were prepared to be grateful for very small mercies. During that time forty-six of the hundred and one settlers had died, and had been buried on the bluff overlooking the landing. All had suffered from cold, hunger, sickness, and fear; and death from the plague had taken away nearly half their numbers. They had lived for a time half-frozen, for their common house had burned. One of their number has given us some of the minor trials which were borne, saying that they were lost in the woods, they had been terrified by the roar of " Lyons," had met wolves that " sat on thier tayles and grinned " at them, and had been horribly frightened by the wild whoop of Indians and the flourish of tomahawks.

These people had become accustomed to fasting, and the recollection of the " Feast of

Farewell " given to the Pilgrims by their friends of Leyden, on the eve of their departure from Holland, was found not sufficient to satisfy the pains of hunger. In the fall of 1621 the men of Plymouth had gathered their crops from twenty acres of corn and six acres of barley and peas; the cold weather had brought into the harbor an abundance of game, and deer and other animals were found in the forests near the settlement. Governor Bradford specified that during that autumn, " beside water-foule, ther was great store of wild turkies." About this time Governor Bradford gave direction for the observance of a day of thanksgiving to be held December thirteenth, 1621. Edward Winslow described this event in strong but simple language:

" Our harvests being gathered in, our governor sent four men on a fowling, so that we might after a special manner rejoice together after we had gathered the fruit of our labors. They four killed in one day as much fowl as, with a little help beside, served the company almost a week. At which time, amongst other recreations, we exercised our arms, many of the Indians coming amongst us, and among the rest their greatest king, Massasoit, with some ninety of his men, whom for three days we entertained and feasted; and they (*i. e.* the Indians) went out and killed five deer, which they brought to the plantation and bestowed on our governor, and upon our captain (Standish), and others; and although it be not always so plentiful as it was at this time with us, yet by the goodness of God we are so far from want that we often wish you were partakers of our plenty."

Governor Bradford, in his famous " History of the Plymouth Colony," tells us of this " plenty " in a more specific way. We also see from his account, the great unselfishness and fine spirit of hospitality among the colonists. "They began now to gather in ye small harvest they had, and to fitte up their houses and dwellings against winter, being all well recovered in health & strength, and had all things in good plenty; for as some were thus employed in affairs abroad, others were exercised in fishing, about codd, & bass, & other fish, of which y^ey tooke good store, of which every family had their portion.

"All ye somer ther was no wante. And now begane to come in store of foule, as winter approached, of which this place did abounde, when they came first (but afterward decreased by degrees). And of these they took many, besides venison. Besides they had aboute a peck of meale a weeke to a person, or now since harvest, Indian corne to y^t proportion. Which made many afterwards write so largely of their plenty hear to their friends in England, which were not fained, but true reports.

" In Novemb^r, about y^t time twelfe month that them selves came, ther came in a small ship to them unexpected or looked for, in which came Mr Cushman and with him 35 persons to remaine & live in ye plantation; which did not a little rejoice them. And they when they came a shore, and found all well, and saw plenty of vitails in every house, were no less glade. For most of them were lusty yonge men, and many of them wild enough, who little considered whither, or aboute what, they wente, till they came into ye harbore at Cap-Codd. So they were all landed; but ther was not so much as a bisket-cake or any other victialls for them, neither had they any beding, but some sory things they had in their cabins, nor pot, nor pan, nor overmany cloaths. The plantation was glad of this addition of strenght but could have wished that many of them had been of better condition; but y^t could not now be helpte."

Umbagt

An Early Th

Massasoit's T

There were but fifty-five English people to eat this first Thanksgiving feast of the Pilgrims, yet with the ninety Indians there were plenty to provide for. There were only four women in the colony, who, with the help of one servant and a few young girls, prepared the food for three days for a hundred and twenty men, three-fourths of whom were Indians, whose capacity for gorging was unequalled.

What courage and good faith they had to celebrate in this way! for they had little cause to rejoice. This little company of stern men, armed, surrounded by savages who were gorgeous in holiday paint and feathers, and a few overworked, sad, homesick women, were trying to forget the weary months of hard work and disappointment, and were bent upon a common enjoyment of the gifts nature had provided, for which they gave hearty thanks to God.

From Governor Bradford and Mr. Winslow we have, probably, a true and reasonable account of this first Plymouth Thanksgiving; but there are other historians who would give us very wonderful reports of conditions and events. We are told by a historian of the day of the " comfortable warm water " which was drank freely.

What this " comfortable " drink was, we are not told, but a Pilgrim Thanksgiving feast cannot be thought of as being accompanied with much carousing or drunkenness. Perhaps the imaginative chronicler who mentions " comfortable warm water " was of the same order as Thomas Morton, who, in his wonderful book, " The New England Canaan," makes the Massachusetts wilderness a land flowing with milk and honey.

His menu of the Puritan feast would have included turkey in every form, lobster, salad and bisque, bear-steak, chops, roast, whole or quartered, — and how easily caught and prepared!

Morton says: " Turkies there are, which divers times in great flocks have sallied by our doores; and then a gunne (being commonly in redinesse) salutes them with such a courtesie, as makes them take a turne in the Cooke room. They daunce by the doore so well! Of these there hath bin killed, that have weighed forty-eight pound a piece. . . . The Beare is a tyrant at a lobster, and at low water will downe to the Rocks, and groape after them with great diligence. Hee will runne away from a man like a little dogge. If a couple of Salvages chance to espie him at his banquet, his running away will not serve his turne, for they will coate him and chase him betweene them home to their houses, where they kill him, to save a laboure in carrying him farre."

Morton's Canaan more than blossomed as the rose — even the rattlesnakes were harmless. He says that his " dogge was venomed with troubling one of these, and so swelled that I had thought it would have bin his death; but with one Saucer of Salat oyle poured downe his throat he has recovered by the next day. Therefore it is a simplicity in any one that shall tell bug beare tales of horribile or terrible Serpents that are in this land."

CHRISTMAS

CHRISTMAS

"A thousand bells ring out, and throw
  Their joyous peals abroad, and smite
  The darkness, charmed and holy now!
  The night that erst no name had worn,
  To it a happy name is given;
  For in that stable lay, new-born,
  The peaceful Prince of earth and heaven,
    In the solemn midnight
      Centuries ago!"

CHRISTMAS

"In furry pall yclad,
His brow enwreathed with holly never sere,
Old Christmas comes to close the waning year."
— BAMPFYLDE.

IN all the year there is no day which fills the heart of the world with such joy and tenderness as Christmas. It is the time when the fire of generous impulse burns high, and, whatever may be said of the danger of Christmas giving being degenerated into mere commercial give-and-take, it is still a pure pleasure to thousands who love children and pity the poor in the spirit of Him in honor of whose birth the day is celebrated.

During the centuries since Christmas first

came to be observed in the Church, the festival has had many severe trials, being condemned and flouted by some, made occasion of gross and sacrilegious riotings and unbridled revelry by others, and at times studiously ignored by those not in sympathy with its upholders.

The customs of Christmas, aside from those directly bearing upon the birth of Christ, are, like so many of our festive rites, adapted from the pagans, who could not have been expected to leave their established habits and change to new ones on becoming Christians, or, if they were expected to, did not, but had such a powerful influence on those who converted them, that the festivals of all subsequent years have reflected their temper.

When Pope Gregory sent St. Augustine to convert Saxon England, he told him to accommodate, as far as possible, Christian to heathen ceremonies, that the people might not be startled; and in particular he advised him to allow them, on certain festivals, to kill and eat "a great number of oxen to the glory of God the Father," as they had done in honor of the devil. On the Christmas next after the arrival of Augustine, he baptized many thousands, but permitted the usual celebration, only prohibiting the intermingling of Christians and pagans in the dances.

The adaptation of pagan to Christian customs is particularly true of Christmas, as many of the ancient Christmas practices were taken from the Roman feast of Saturn. The Puritan author of the "Historia Mastix" was not far wrong when he wrote: "If we compare our Bacchanalian Christmasses with these Saturnalia, we shall find such a near affinitye between them, both in regard to time and in manner of solemnizing, that we must needs conclude the one be but the very issue of the other."

Some communities of Christians used to celebrate the sixth of January, others the twenty-ninth of March, others the twenty-fifth of December, but about the year 340, Pope Julius I. fixed the date as December twenty-fifth, and now all nations of Christians celebrate the same day.

During the Middle Ages the Church was in the fullest splendor of its power. Gothic architecture had attained its highest perfection, painting and sculpture were almost exclusively devoted to the decoration of churches, the liturgical works were rich in poetry and music, and the Christmas celebration was gorgeously beautiful, both in Church, ceremonial, and social custom.

But later the festival degenerated into a mere occasion for vulgar riot and lawlessness. On Christmas Eve the streets were so filled with such a rough, boisterous crowd that passage was almost impossible. With drinking, gambling, shouts of vile revel, and vulgar songs, the *Lord of Misrule* and his companions held full sway, and none dared, or cared, to interfere.

Master Stubbs, the Puritan, in his characteristic way, describes this horse-play of the time; and it is said that he has not exaggerated it.

" All the wild heads of the parish flocking together, choose them a grand captain of Mischief, whome they enoble with the title of *Lord of Misrule;* and him they crown with great solemnity and adopt for their king. This king anointed, chooseth four, twenty, forty, three-score, or an hundred like himself to wait upon his lordly Majesty, and to guard his noble person.

" Then every one of these men he investeth with his liveries of green, of yellow, or some other light wanton color; and as though they were not gaudy enough, they bedeck themselves with scarves, ribbons, and laces, hung all over with gold rings, precious stones, and other jewels.

" This done, they tie about either leg twenty or forty bells, with rich handkerchiefs on their heads, and sometimes laid across their shoulders and necks.

" Then have they their hobby-horses, their dragons, and other antics, together with their bawdy pipes and thundering drummers to strike the devil's dance withal.

" Then march this heathenish company to the church, their pipes piping, their drums thundering, their bells jingling, their hand-kerchiefs fluttering about their heads like madmen, their hobby-horses and other monsters skirmishing among the throng. And in this sort they go to church though minister be at prayer or preaching, — dancing and singing with such a confused noise that no man can hear his own voice. And these terrestrial furies spend the Sabbath day.

" Then they have certain papers wherein

is printed some babelerie or other imaginary work, and these they call my Lord of Misrule's badges. These they give to every one that will give them money to maintain them in their heathenish devilry. And who will not show himself buxom to them, and give them money, he shall be mocked and flouted shamefully, — yea, and many times carried on a cow-staff and dived over head and ears in water or otherwise most horribly abused."

These holy-day frolics seem to have been indulged in at first by the common people, but the clergy and magistrates connived at these rude ceremonials, and churches were given up to their revels and mock services, which consisted of imitations of sacred rites, and parodies on the hymns of the church.

An effort was made to reform these practices, but they had taken too firm a hold on the people. The spirit of the times was not above such desecrations, and those who protested were thrown into prison.

As the Protestant spirit gained among the people, the antagonism which arose toward the Church became bitter indeed, and all Church-days and holy-days were strictly disregarded.

One of the popular *Rump ballads* at the time of the reaction from the rule of Cromwell, expresses the feeling with which Protestants were regarded by their opponents, for not observing Christmas and other holidays:

> "But such have been these times of late,
>   That holy-days are out of date,
>   And holynesse to boote;
>   For they that do despise and scorn
>   To keep the day that Christ was born
>   Want holynesse, no doubt."

At the time of the Reformation the Calvinists rejected the celebration of Christmas absolutely, and the clergy in Scotland tried to throw contempt on the day. It is said that they made their wives and servants spin and weave, and their tenants to yoke their oxen to the plough; but John Hamilton says that " Our Lord has not left it unpunisit: for their oxen ran mad and brake their nekis and lamed sum pleughmen, as is notoriously knawin in sundrie partes of Scotland."

Even in the midst of fanaticism, however, Christmas festivities could not be entirely abolished, for there were those who celebrated the day without excess, in mere gaiety of heart, without the least intention of dishonoring religion. In the " Vindication of Christmas," old Father Christmas, complaining of his treatment under Puritan rule, says: " But, welcome or not, I am come," — and he came to stay. He says further that his best welcome was from some Devonshire farmers. " After dinner, we rose from the boord, and sate by the fire, where the harth was imbrodered all over with roasted apples piping hot, excepting a bole of ale for a cooler, after which we discoursed merily;

some went to cards, others sang carols and
pleasant songs suitable to the times: then
the poor laboring hinds and maid-servants,
with the ploughboys, went nimbly to dancing, the poor toyling wretches being glad
of my company, because they had little or
no sport at all till I came amongst them;
and therefore they skipped and leaped for
joy, singing a carol to the tune of *hey:*

"Let's dance and sing and make good cheer,
    For Christmas comes but once a year.
    Draw hogsheads dry, let flagons fly,
    For now the bells shall ring;
    Whilst we endeavor to make good
    The title 'gainst the king."

So in spite of the changes of Church and
state, the Christmas spirit ruled in every
heart, and the day was observed in some way
according to the rank and temper of the
individual.

There are many customs connected with
the celebration of Christmas which have
been followed for centuries. That of dec-

orating houses and churches with ever-greens is of very ancient date, the tradi-tional plants being box, fir, holly, and mistle-toe; and all these are still in demand. The fir Christmas-tree was first used by the Germans, and from them it was introduced into England.

The ancient Druids went in solemn pro-cession to the annual cutting of mistletoe on the sixth day of the moon nearest New Year's. The officiating priest, clad in white robes and carrying a golden sickle, cut the plant, which was received on a white cloth. To add to the impressiveness, bulls, and even human victims, were offered in its honor. Mistletoe was supposed to keep away witches, and the people accordingly paid the Druids large sums for a piece of it to hang around their necks for a charm. There is an old superstition that to hold a sprig of mistletoe in the hand will not only enable one to see ghosts, but will force them to speak to him; and, according to tradition, the maid not kissed beneath the mistletoe at Christmas will go without a husband another year.

The use of greens for decoration is seen in this old English description, which has a mixture of superstition: "Against the feast of Christmas, every man's house, as also their parish churches, were decked with Holm, Iuy, Bays, and whatsoeuer the season of the yeere aforded to be greene. The Conduits and Standards of the streetes were likewise garnished. Amongst the which, I read that in the yeere 1444, by tempest of thunder and lightening, Paul's steeple was fiered, but with great labour quenched, and toward morning a Standard of tree being set up in the midst of the pauement, fast in the ground, nayled full of Holme and Iuy, for the disport of Christmas to the people, was torn up and cast downe by a malignant Spirit (as was thought), and the stones of the pauement all about were cast in the streets, and into divers houses, so that the people were sore aghast at the Tempest."

The high regard in which holly was held is expressed in this old Saxon couplet:

> " Whosoever against holly do cry .
> In a rope shall be hung full high.
> Alleulia ! "

And a well-known fifteenth-century carol begins:

> " Holly and Ivy, Box and Bay
> Put in the church on Christmas Day."

Decorations remained in churches and dwellings till Candlemas Day, when they must all be taken down, for people had superstitions about their remaining longer. Herrick alludes to this popular prejudice in the lines:

> " Down with the rosemary, and so
> Down with the baies and mistletoe;
> Down with the holly, ivie, all
> Wherewith ye drest the Christmas Hall;

That, so the superstitious find
No one least branch there left behind;
For look how many leaves there be
Neglected there: Maids, trust to me,
So many goblins you will see."

The Yule-log is a remnant of the *Juul,*
when the Scandinavians used to kindle huge
fires in the honor of their god Thor.

In some parts of old England, bringing
in the Yule-log was the principal ceremony
of Christmas Eve, and was welcomed with
song and sport. These stanzas, found in the
Sloane Manuscripts, are supposed to be of
the time of Henry VI.:

"Welcome be Thou, heavenly King,
Welcome, bairn on this morning,
Welcome, for whom we shall sing
　　　　　Welcome Yule.

"Welcome be ye, Stephen and John:
Welcome innocents every one;
Welcome Thomas Martyr one
　　　　　Welcome Yule.

"Welcome be ye that are here:
　　Welcome all, and make good cheer;
　　Welcome all another year
　　　　　　Welcome Yule."

Part of the log was carefully preserved to light the Yule-log of the succeeding year. It was believed that a piece of the log in the house was a security against fire; and if a squinting person entered the room while it was burning, all sorts of ill-luck would come to the family.

A Yule-candle of enormous size was lighted, which burned on the table at supper, and in the buttery of St. John's College, Oxford, an ancient candle-socket of stone still remains. It was thought that nothing added more to the cheer of the company than plenty of warmth and light, and both were particularly welcome to the peasants who were entertained with a dinner at the landlord's house. It was the old English custom for the serfs to bring a load of wood with them, and their dinner was to last the length of time that it took "to burn away a *wet wheel*" on the open fire in the hall, in which the meal took place. As this "wet wheel" (which was simply a tree section of green wood) was supplied by the tenants, and their dinner of good things was to last during its burning, we may be sure that each year the "wheel" was cut thicker and thicker till it became a log.

Burning the Yule-log in England in later times was an important ceremony. The log was drawn by servants into the hall, where each member of the family, sitting down in turn on the log, sang a Yule-song, and drank a cup of spiced ale. The log was then cast on the fire with prayers for the safety of the house and the happiness of its inmates until next Yule-tide. Then came a riotous time when the spirit of misrule reigned. Pleasures were provided for all, Yule-cakes, barrels of ale, dancing, singing, romping, laughing, kissing under the mistletoe, more eating and drinking; then gathering around the blazing log to tell legendary tales till the bells of midnight gave warning that it was time to disperse.

In Herrick's rollicking verse is a picture of a Yule-log company:

"Come bring with a noise
  My merry, merry boys,
    The Christmas log to the firing.
  While my good dame she
  Bids ye all be free
    And drink to your heart's desiring.

"With the last year's brand
  Light the new block, and
    For good success in his spending,
  On your psalteries play,
  That sweet luck may
    Come while the log is tending."

In Poor Robin's Almanack for 1677, he observes for Christmas Day:

"Now blocks to cleave
  This time requires,

'Gainst Christmas for
To make good fires."

A halo of superstition seems to surround
Christmas Eve, and people liked to believe
that the oxen knelt in the stalls in adoration,
that bells were heard from under the earth,
that bees hummed Christmas hymns in their
hives, and the cock sang all the night
through.   Marcellus says, in Hamlet:

" Some say
That ever 'gainst the season comes ,
Wherein our Saviour's birth is celebrated,
The bird of dawning singeth all night long;
And then, they say, no spirit can walk abroad,
The nights are wholesome; then no planets strike,
No fairy takes, no witch hath power to charm,
So hallowed and so gracious is the time."

A famous Christmas wonder is the thorn-
tree which blossoms every Christmas Day.
According to the legend, St. Joseph of Ari-
mathea landed not far from the town of
Glastonbury, England, and stuck his staff
into the ground while he rested himself.

The stick took root and budded afterward every Christmas. The tree was cut down by a Puritan, but we are told that he cut his leg during the chopping, and a chip flew up and put out his right eye.

The trunk of this wonderful tree, though separated from the root, grew and flourished, and slips were planted elsewhere so that blossoms were taken abroad, and sold as relics to merchants, at fabulous prices.

Mumming and masking were favorite Christmas amusements in the olden time, and are probably remnants of the Roman Masquerades.

About the twelfth century miracle plays were introduced, and London became famous for them. Although full of anachronisms, these plays were none the less entertaining to the people, who were easily pleased. Noah's wife refuses to go into the ark, and swears by St. John; when forced in, she salutes Noah with a box on the ear.

Pharaoh, in his pursuit of the Israelites, when in fear of drowning, recommends his people to lift up their hearts to Mahomet. Noah's wife swears by Mary, Caiaphas sings mass, and the wondering shepherds are acquainted with the wise men of Gotham.

In 1377 a splendid masquerade was performed by the citizens of London before the Black Prince, and again twelve aldermen with their sons visited Henry IV. as mummers. Henry VIII. passed an act declaring mummers liable to be sent to jail as vagabonds, which of course abolished the practice.

Besides public entertainments, there were various sports and games for the family. A list of games given in Burton's " Anatomy of Melancholy " not only shows a little contradiction of contents and title of the ancient book, but shows us also that people were well supplied with Christmas amusements. There were " cardes, dice, chesse, shovel-

board, the philosopher's game, small tremkes,
shuttlecock, musicke, masks, singing, dancing, jests, riddles, merry tales, etc." There
was also mention of " jugglers and jack-
puddings, post and pair, hot cockles," and
other games now obsolete.

There were always the pleasures of a
Christmas dinner, and these were by no
means slight. The typical bill of fare included " good drink, pudding, souce, and
mustard (which is a provoker of noble
thirst), beef, mutton, pig, veal, goose, capon
and turkey, apples and nuts." Poor Robin, in
his Almanack for 1700, thinks feasting and
Christmas should go hand in hand:

> " Now that the time has come wherein
>   Our Saviour Christ was born,
> The larder's full of beef and pork,
>   The garner's full of corn;
> As God hath plenty to thee sent,
>   Take comfort of thy labors,
> And let it never thee repent
>   To feast thy needy neighbors."

A rhymster has dilated humorously on the menu of a Christmas dinner of the olden time:

"They served up salmon, venison and wild boars
   By hundreds and by dozens and by scores, .
Hogsheads of honey, kilderkins of mustard,
Muttons and fatted beeves, and bacon swine,
Herons and bitterns, peacocks, swan and bustard,
Teal, mallard, pigeons, widgeons and in fine
Plum puddings, pancakes, apple-pies and custard,
And therewithal they drank good Gascon wine,
With mead, and ale and cider of our own,
For porter, punch and negus were not known."

A boar's head was essential to a well-regulated Christmas dinner, and was not only considered very good eating but ornamental as well.

A student of Queen's College, Oxford, is said to have been walking in Shotover Forest, studying Aristotle, when a boar rushed out at him, but with great presence of mind he crammed the book down the beast's throat and choked it. Of course, a

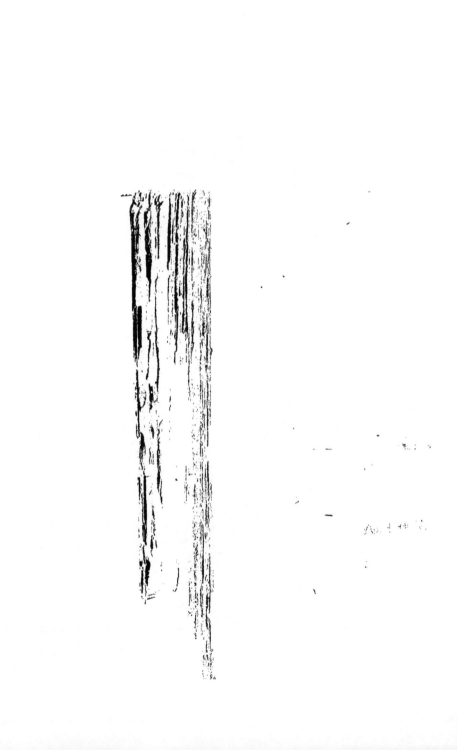

poor student could not waste a good Aristotle by losing it in the neck of a boar, so the head was cut off and the book recovered. But a good boar's head could not be wasted any more than a classic tome, so it was taken to the college and was roasted and eaten. This is said to have been the origin of the dish in the college.

The lessee of the tithes of Horn Church, Essex, had to provide, every Christmas, a boar's head to be wrestled for in a field adjoining the church; the victor was expected to invite his companions to dinner, so that each got his share of roast pig's head.

Another popular dish was a peacock roasted and decorated with feathers. If oaths were taken, it was with drawn swords held over the bird, and the words " By cock and pie " used.

Whatever else was served, there must be a plum-pudding and mince pies; and we find recipes for these essentials in the "Whole Body of Cookery Dissected," for 1675.

These feastings were abhorred by the Puritans, and their plain living has been the subject for doggerel:

> "The high-shoe lords of Cromwell's making,
>   Were not for dainties, roasting, baking;
>   The chiefest food they found most good in,
>   Was rusty bacon and bag pudding;
>   Plum broth was papish, and mince pie —
>   Oh, that was flat idolatry!"

It is said that a Puritan declared that:

> "All plums the prophet's sons deny,
>   And spice-broths are too hot:
>   Treason's in December pie,
>   And death within the pot."

Christmas is remembered in the different countries of Europe according to their peculiar national characteristics. The Norwegian makes much of the virtue of hospitality, and the first courtesy is to offer a pipe of

tobacco, and at dinner, which is simpler
than among other people, national hymns
are sung between the courses. No nation
in the world can surpass Norway in its en-
thusiastic love of country, and patriotic
songs are in order even at a Christmas dinner.

In Sweden, where cleanliness is nearer
godliness than anywhere else, the houses are
completely renovated for the Christmas festival. An almost universal custom is that
of tying a sheaf of corn to a pole, which
is placed in the garden for the birds' Christmas dinner.

At Christmas time the Italians prepare
for themselves sumptuous banquets, mostly
of fish, done in wonderful and diverse ways;
and fish is eaten a week before the great
feast night. Churches are largely attended
at this season as the religious feature is
emphasized. At home entertainments, the
girls and boys vie with each other in showing

off their accomplishments, and reciting what
has been learned expressly for the day, to
please and surprise their parents. Con-
spicuous among the presents is the " urn
of fate." Children and friends in order of
their age are bidden to put their hands into
the urn and draw their lot. Many a blank
is drawn, but in the end each one is satisfied with what best suits him. This urn
is to the Italian children what the Christmas-
tree is to the young people of other countries.

It is from the Germans that we have
taken the Christmas-tree, and from them we
have learned to observe our social Christmas with more reference to the children.
The home Christmas in Germany is the characteristic one, when all thought is for the
pleasure of the home circle.

The first century of Colonial life in America saw few days for pleasures. The holy-
days appointed by the English Church were
unsavory to the Puritan nostrils, and their

public celebration was strictly forbidden by the laws of New England; new holidays were not quickly established, the sober church gatherings being thought recreation enough.

The hatred of " wanton Bacchanalian Christmasses " described by Cotton as a time of " revelling, dicing, carding, masking, and mumming, consumed in compotations, in interludes, in excess of wine, in mad mirth," was but a reaction against the excesses of the festival led by the lord of misrule.

The Pilgrims were so anxious to " beate down every sprout of Episcopacie," that they frowned down any attempt at celebrating a holiday which had been countenanced by the English Church. A Plymouth Pilgrim wrote in his diary: " 1620, Monday the 25, being Christmas Day, we went on shore, some to fell tymber, some to saw, some to rine, and some to carry, so no man rested all that day; but towards night, some, as they were at worke, heard a noyse of some

Indians, which caused vs all to goe to our Muskets, but we heard no further, so we came aboord againe, and left some twentie to keep the court of gard. We began to drink water aboord, but at night the Master caused vs to have some Beere, and so on board we had diverse times, now and then some Beere, but on shore none at all."

This was a very frugal Christmas indeed; but in those days everything was frugal, and people were thankful for little pleasures.

Governor Bradford wrote in his diary: "Y^e 25 day, begane to erect ye first house for comone use to receive them and their goods;" and years later Christmas celebrations had not made much headway, as will be seen by an entry in a Puritan diary: "December 25, 1685. Carts come to town and shops open as usual. Some somehow observe the day, but are vexed. I believe that the Body of people profane it, and blessed be God no authority yet to compel them to keep it."

Christmas Day as it now exists contains elements of the old-time customs, which are modified and refined. There is fervor in church service, without fanaticism; there is great hospitality, yet the poor are not for·gotten, and withal, in this semi-religious, semi-festive season are gaieties, reunion of friends, giving of presents, and an exchange of compliments.

The Christmas customs in America have been transplanted from Europe: our Christmas-tree comes from Germany, our Santa Claus from Holland, the Christmas-stocking from Belgium or France, while " Merry Christmas " was the old English greeting shouted from window to street on Christmas morning.

All nations will have their enjoyments, and, if they contain a religious element, they appeal to all classes. Christmas has ever

been the most important Christian festival
in the calendar, and in many countries, amid
all the pleasures of the time, the true spirit
of charity is expressed. A striking example
of this is the Yule-peace of the Scandinavians, which lasts from Christmas to Epiphany, and is proclaimed by the public crier.
Any violation of the Yule-peace is visited
with double punishment; the courts are
closed, old quarrels are adjusted, and old
feuds are forgotten. Other, more spontaneous, examples may be seen in the care of
the poor, and especially of poor children at
Christmas time; in this is shown the Christ
spirit; for with him there was no prejudice,
nor social tradition; he kept in the company
of those who needed him, while the social
classes of his generation could not understand his preference for publicans and sin-
ners instead of saints and Pharisees.

We cannot estimate the extent of influence which art has had in giving color

to our Christmas thought. The great artists
have given us their conception of the na-
tivity, and these in turn have influenced our
imaginations, and form a vital part of our
associations with Christmas. The frescoed
walls of churches, the bas-reliefs, the carved
pulpits and shrines, the beautiful colored
windows — all the pictorial conceptions of
the early artists help to fix the event of
Christ's birth in the popular mind.

The modern thought in the celebration of
this event seems to tend toward a healthy
condition of love toward, and confidence in,
our brother men; and while we hold the
religious idea, we may sing and dance without fearing that the earth will open and
swallow us up, but may be sure that whatever objectionable features there are now
will die out naturally under the influence of
reason and progress, and a greater infusion
of the Christ spirit.

The birth of Christ has always been a

favorite theme for song and verse. Many
very early Christmas carols are preserved
in the British Museum. A collection of
carols was published as early as 1521; another ancient collection is entitled, " Cer-
tayne goodly Carowles to be songe to the
Glory of God," and another, " Chrestenmas
Carowles auctorisshed by my lord of London."

Milton, in " Paradise Lost," alludes to the
first Christmas carol :

"His place of birth a solemn angel tells
  To simple shepherds keeping watch by night;
  They gladly thither haste, and by a quire
  Of squadroned angels hear his carol sung."

Here is a carol of the time of Henry VI. :

"Lystenyl, lordyngs, more and lees,
  I bryng you tydyns of gladnes,
  As Gabriel beryt wytnes,
                    dicam vobis quia.

"I bring you tydynges that fwul goude,
Now es borne a blyesful foude
That bowt us alle upon the rode,
sua morte pia.

"For the trespas of Adam,
Fro ys fader Jhesu ho cam
Here in herthe how kende he man,
sua mente pia.

"Mayde moder, swete virgine,
Was godnys nay no man divine
Sche bare a schild wyt wot pyne,
teste profecia.

"Marie moder, that ys so fre,
Wyt herte mylde y pray to the,
Fro the fende thou kepe me,
tua price pia."

A very curious specimen in the Scottish language is preserved in " Ane compendious Booke of godly and spiritual Sangs " :

"ANE SANG OF THE BIRTH OF CHRIST
WITH THE TUNE OF BALULALOW

"I come from Hevin to tell
The best nowellis that ever befell;
To you this thythinges trew I bring,
And I will of them say and sing.

· " This day to you is borne ane Child,
Of Marie meike and Virgine mylde,
That blissit Barne, bining and kynde,
Sall you rejoyce baith heart and mynde.

" My saull and lyfe, stand up and see
Quha lyes in ane cribe of tree,
Quhat Babe is that, so gude and faire?
It is Christ, God's sonne and aire.

" O God! that made all creature,
How art thou becum so pure,
That on the hay and stray will lye,
Amang the asses, oxin, and kye?

" O, my deir hert, zoung Jesus sweit,
Prepare thy creddle in my spreit,
And I sall rocke thee in my hert,
And never mair from thee depart.

" But I sall praise thee ever moir,
With sangs sweit unto thy gloir.
The knees of my hert sall I bow,
And sing that right Balulalow."

THE END.

Lightning Source UK Ltd.
Milton Keynes UK
UKHW010947180119
335792UK00009B/289/P

9 781330 720318